PROTECT YOUR NEST EGG FROM THE
NURSING HOME:
YOUR FLORIDA SURVIVAL GUIDE

D. "REP" DELOACH III
ESTATE PLANNING AND BOARD CERTIFIED ELDER LAW ATTORNEY

WORD ASSOCIATION PUBLISHERS
www.wordassociation.com
1.800.827.7903

Copyright © 2018 by D. "Rep" DeLoach III

All rights reserved. No part of this book/manuscript may be reproduced in any form or by any electronic or mechanical means, including information or storage and retrieval systems, without permission in writing from the author.

Printed in the United States of America.

ISBN: 978-1-63385-283-9

Designed and published by

Word Association Publishers
205 Fifth Avenue
Tarentum, Pennsylvania 15084

www.wordassociation.com
1.800.827.7903

A NOTE FROM D. "REP" DELOACH III

IF YOU ARE reading this, you may be concerned about how long-term care will affect you, your loved one, your assets and your family. ***Protect Your Nest Egg from the Nursing Home: Your Florida Survival Guide*** is designed to help you prepare for you or your loved one's financial future. Many people are afraid of running out of money in their old age, even if they have significant assets. Others may want to make sure their heirs receive an inheritance instead of their funds disappearing to the very high cost of nursing home care. In working with the elderly and their families for almost two decades, I understand that planning for long-term care, either for yourself or for a family member, can be very confusing as there are few places to get good answers for your specific situation.

In writing this book, I want to set the law out as plainly as possible, dispelling myths and giving good, practical advice. As in most matters of life, the fear of the unknown may be the most difficult part in any given situation.

Please note that the discussion of Medicaid throughout this book applies to Medicaid used to pay for long-term care, such as in the nursing home, at home or in the assisted living facility. Medicaid has many different programs with different rules for qualification. Here, we will discuss qualification only for the Florida long-term care programs.

If you want to learn more about good estate planning, including wills, trusts and probate, please read my book, *The Top 20 Ways to Protect Your Florida Estate*.

The aging process has enough worries and difficulties – hopefully this book will set some of these basic matters straight so that you and your loved ones can make the best decisions in preparing for the future.

Sincerely,

D. "Rep" DeLoach III
Board Certified in Elder Law, Florida Bar

LEGAL DISCLAIMER

Of course, a legal book written by an attorney must have a disclaimer. Here is ours:

This book will be a great help in helping you understand the practical, legal and financial aspects of aging, particularly how it relates to receiving long-term care. Of course, the material is provided for informational purposes only. It is not to be considered or construed as rendering legal advice. The reader should consult an experienced elder law attorney to review his or her own specific situation.

ACKNOWLEDGEMENT

Chapters 7, 8 and 9 of this book were written by Don Quante, a financial planner. Don Quante is one of the leading financial planners in helping families protect their assets from the nursing home. Don's financial company, America's First Financial Corp., works with attorneys and their clients in helping pre-plan to protect assets from the high cost of long-term care.

DEDICATION

This book is dedicated to some of the most important people in my life:

My elder law team, including Tammy, Gloria, Best, Mary Lou, Ashleigh, Lorry, April, Becky and Christine, all of whom make my life better on a daily basis;

My father, Dennis R. DeLoach, Jr., who founded our law firm in 1976, who still works full time, and is a continuing inspiration on how a good attorney should act and treat his clients; and

My beloved wife, Simone, who works as our law firm's director of marketing. Bringing her into our law firm was one of the best decisions I could have ever made.

TABLE OF CONTENTS

Meet Sally, Our Typical Client 13

Section 1: Long-Term Care and How It Will Affect You 15
    Chapter 1: Will You (Or Your Loved One) Need
        Long-Term Care? 16
    Chapter 2: Different Types of Long-Term Care 21
    Chapter 3: How to Find a Good Long-Term Care
        Facility 28
    Chapter 4: Long-Term Care Can Be Very Expensive 35

Section 2: What to Know Before You Need Long-Term Care ... 39
    Chapter 5: Staying at Home for as Long as Possible 40
    Chapter 6: Long-Term Care Insurance and You 49
    Chapter 7: Annuity-Based Long-Term Care and
        The Pension Protection Act of 2006
        by Don Quante 57
    Chapter 8: Life Insurance/Long-Term Care Strategy
        by Don Quante 60
    Chapter 9: Asset-Based Long-Term Care Strategy
        by Don Quante 62
    Chapter 10: Understanding Health Insurance:
        Medicare and HMOs 67

Section 3: Government Benefits and Long-Term Care 75
    Chapter 11: Medicaid and Long-Term Care 76
    Chapter 12: Veterans Benefits and Long-Term Care 94
    Chapter 13: Common Questions and Answers on
        Medicaid and VA Benefits 103

Section 4: Pre-Planning for Long-Term Care 115

Chapter 14: Incapacity Planning: Durable Powers of Attorney and Advance Directives 116

Chapter 15: Who to Name in Your Incapacity Documents 124

Chapter 16: Irrevocable Trust Planning Five Years Before You Need Medicaid 128

Section 5: Finding Help 135

Chapter 17: Choosing the Right Attorney for You 136

Chapter 18: Finding Local Services 137

Chapter 19: My Elder Just Went to the Nursing Home: What Should I Do Next? 139

Glossary of Elder Law Terms 145

About the Author 161

MEET SALLY
OUR TYPICAL CLIENT

THROUGHOUT THIS BOOK we will be referring to our typical client, Sally, and how the long-term care process will affect her and her family.

Early one Monday morning, we receive a phone call from a client's frantic daughter. Our client, Sally, age 93, recently fell and went to the hospital for five days with a broken hip. Sally is now in the skilled nursing facility receiving rehabilitation. Sally had been doing fairly well at home alone but she had slowed down a little in recent years. Her daughter had noticed that Sally was getting more forgetful but Sally had brushed off any thoughts of dementia.

Now in the rehabilitation facility, Sally does not want to participate in getting stronger. Her dementia has also gotten worse and she is not able to remember her directions from the physical therapist. Up until this point, Sally's Medicare is paying for her rehabilitation but the family has been told that Sally's rehab will end soon as Sally is not participating in rehab. The facility says that Sally cannot go home as she will be unsafe.

Sally's daughter is extremely concerned about her mother. She has so many questions and does not know where to go and what to do. Her questions are:

- Will Sally be able to go home with helpers at home?
- Where will Sally go if she cannot go home?
- Can Sally to go assisted living? If so, which one?
- Will Sally need to stay in the nursing home? Will this facility accept her?
- Will Sally get good care in her new facility?
- How will Sally pay for her long-term care? The daughter has heard that both the nursing home and assisted living are expensive.
- Can her daughter protect Sally's assets and apply for Medicaid?
- Sally's husband was a WWII veteran – can this help pay for Sally's care?
- What about that $5,000 gift that Sally gave to her family at Christmas?
- How will her daughter access Sally's bank accounts and pay her bills?
- What will be done with Sally's home and car if she is not safe at home?
- Will all of Sally's money disappear to the nursing home?

These are the typical questions a family will experience, and more, when they are experiencing a loved one's decline. This book will attempt to navigate you through the long-term care process and how it could affect you or your loved one.

SECTION 1:
LONG-TERM CARE AND HOW IT WILL AFFECT YOU

Chapter 1:
Will You (Or Your Loved One) Need Long-Term Care?

Chapter 2:
Different Types of Long-Term Care

Chapter 3:
How to Find a Good Long-Term Care Facility

Chapter 4:
Long-Term Care Can Be Very Expensive

CHAPTER 1

WILL YOU (OR YOUR LOVED ONE) NEED LONG-TERM CARE?

WE ALL WANT to live a healthy, long life and have a peaceful death after a short illness. The reality is that few of us are able to leave this world quickly and painlessly. As we get older, there is a greater likelihood that we will have a physical or mental decline that will affect our ability to live alone and at home. Chronic illness such as osteoporosis, Parkinson's, COPD, congestive heart failure and others affect our ability to live without constant medical care. Further, Alzheimer's, old age and other types of dementia may affect us as well. The odds of having one of these conditions only increase as we get older, which affects our needs for long-term care.

WHAT IS LONG-TERM CARE?

Long-term care is a **range of services and support** you may need to meet your personal care needs. Most long-term care is not medical care, but rather assistance with the basic personal tasks of everyday life, sometimes called Activities of Daily Living (ADLs), such as:

- Bathing
- Dressing
- Using the toilet
- Transferring (to or from bed or chair)

- Caring for incontinence
- Eating

Other common long-term care services and supports are assistance with everyday tasks, sometimes called Instrumental Activities of Daily Living (IADLs) including:

- Housework
- Managing money
- Taking medication
- Preparing and cleaning up after meals
- Shopping for groceries or clothes
- Using the telephone or other communication devices
- Caring for pets
- Responding to emergency alerts such as fire alarms

Depending upon your need for assistance with ADLs or IADLs, this will determine where you will receive good care and in the correct environment.

WHO WILL NEED LONG-TERM CARE?

70% of people turning age 65 can expect to use some form of long-term care during their lives. There are a number of factors that affect the possibility that you will need care:

Age

- The older you are, the more likely you will need long-term care

Gender
- Women outlive men by about five years on average, so they are more likely to live at home alone when they are older

Disability
- Having an accident or chronic illness that causes a disability is another reason for needing long-term care
- Between ages 40 and 50, on average, eight percent of people have a disability that could require long-term care services
- 69 percent of people age 90 or more have a disability

Health Status
- Chronic conditions such as diabetes and high blood pressure make you more likely to need care
- Your family history such as whether your parents or grandparents had chronic conditions, may increase your likelihood
- Poor diet and exercise habits increase your chances of needing long-term care

Living Arrangements
- If you live alone, you're more likely to need paid care than if you're married, or single, and living with a partner

HOW MUCH CARE WILL YOU NEED?

The duration and level of long-term care will vary from person to person and often change over time. Here are some statistics (all are "on average") you should consider:

WILL YOU (OR YOUR LOVED ONE) NEED LONG-TERM CARE?

- Someone turning age 65 today has almost a 70% chance of needing some type of long-term care services and supports in their remaining years
- Women need care longer (3.7 years) than men (2.2 years)
- One-third of today's 65 year-olds may never need long-term care support, but 20 percent will need it for longer than 5 years

The table below* shows that, overall, more people use long-term care services at home (and for longer) than in facilities.

Type of care	Average number of years people use this type of care	Percent of people who use this type of care (%)
Any Services	3 years	69
At Home		
Unpaid care only	1 year	59
Paid care	Less than 1 year	42
Any care at home	2 years	65
In Facilities		
Nursing facilities	1 year	35
Assisted living	Less than 1 year	13
Any care in facilities	1 year	37

*Source: Long-Term Care.Gov

Key Point to Remember:

> Planning for your eventual long-term care is very important as the odds are that you will become incapacitated before you die.

- While our society is living longer, healthier lives, it is still best to start your planning now, while you can make the best decisions possible.

CHAPTER 2
DIFFERENT TYPES OF LONG-TERM CARE

As in Sally's situation above, when you or your loved one are not able to stay home alone, it can be a very confusing and difficult time. Most people have never dealt with the long-term care of a loved one and are lost. Most do not know the differences between rehabilitation, long-term care, assisted living, dementia care and more. Our first goal is to discuss where long-term care can happen in the event staying home is not an option. Chapter 3 will review the costs for long-term care while Chapter 4 will discuss staying at home for as long as possible.

SKILLED NURSING FACILITY

Often referred to as a "nursing home," a skilled nursing facility (frequently called a "SNF" or "SNIFF" in the industry) offers the highest level of care for the patient. Nursing homes provide custodial and skilled nursing care 24/7. Most people enter a SNF for rehabilitation after a 3 day (or more) hospital stay. When Medicare (and rehabilitation) ends, the patient will either need to go home, go to assisted living, or will need to stay in the SNF for long-term care.

Skilled nursing care involves trained professionals performing services that are needed temporarily or permanently needed, including:

- a nurse attending to a post-operative wound or dispensing and monitoring intravenous medications
- a physical therapist working with a resident to rectify strength and balance issues
- a speech therapist assisting a resident in reclaiming their ability to communicate following a stroke
- an occupational therapist helping a resident to become independent again, particularly when it comes to dressing, personal hygiene and eating
- pharmaceutical, laboratory and radiology services
- social and educational activities
- laundry services
- limited transportation
- end-of-life or hospice care

Most people look to the SNF for care as a last resort as the elder is not able to stay at home alone, or even assisted living, for various reasons. We can generally say that the SNF is reserved for our most frail clients or clients with certain medical needs that cannot be provided at home or in assisted living.

ASSISTED LIVING FACILITY

Most of us would much rather live in an assisted living facility (ALF) than in a nursing home. The ALF more closely resembles your own home, with private and shared units, doors closed for the residents, higher levels of mental/physical function for the residents, more social activities, and more. ALFs are residential care facilities that provide housing, meals, personal care and supportive services to older persons and disabled adults who are unable to live independently. ALFs are intended to be a less costly alternative to more restrictive, institutional settings (i.e., the SNF) for individuals who do not require 24-hour nursing supervision. ALFs are regulated in a manner so as to encourage dignity, individuality, and choice for residents, while providing reasonable assurance for their safety and welfare.

To reside in a standard ALF, a person must meet the standard ALF "residency criteria." The resident's physician must complete a form 1833 for admission into an ALF in Florida. Generally speaking, ALFs provide supervision, assistance with personal and supportive services, and assistance with or administration of medications to elders and disabled adults who require such services.

In addition to a standard ALF license, there are 3 "specialty" licenses in Florida:

- Extended congregate care (ECC),
- Limited nursing services (LNS), and
- Limited mental health (LMH).

An ALF holding an extended congregate care (ECC) license may provide additional nursing services and total assistance with personal care services. Residents living in ECC-licensed facilities may have higher impairment levels than those living in a standard ALF. Residents living in an ALF holding a LNS or LMH license must meet the same residency criteria as a standard-licensed ALF. Consequently, ECC licensed facilities are typically the most expensive ALFs as they provide care that is closest to the nursing home.

Regardless of the facility's license status, residents living in ALFs cannot have conditions that require 24-hour nursing supervision. The only exception is for an existing resident who is receiving licensed hospice services while residing in the ALF, which is discussed further in the "Aging in Place" later in this chapter.

While ALFs generally cost less than nursing facilities, the cost of an ALF varies greatly depending on the location, residential unit size, amenities, and services provided by the facility as discussed in the next chapter.

DEMENTIA CARE ASSISTED LIVING

Many ALFs offer dementia only care. These ALFs may have a segregated, secured unit for dementia care, or they may have the entire facility dedicated to dementia care. Generally, while many ALF residents may have dementia in some form, the specific dementia ALF units feature staff that are all trained to deal with the dementia disease process. Also, the units are designed in certain ways (soothing colors, small rooms) and are secured to prevent wondering from that facility.

SKILLED NURSING CARE VS. ASSISTED LIVING

Choosing between skilled nursing care and assisted living can be difficult. A skilled nursing care facility may be needed if your family member requires:

- round-the-clock nursing care, particularly if the senior might stray if left unsupervised
- assistance with meals, personal hygiene, medications and portability
- more help than the family or present caregiver can provide or the senior can no longer live alone

ALFs are recommended when the senior does not require much medical care but they do need more assistance than can be provided in their home. ALFs:

- allow residents to live independently in their own "apartment"
- provide meals, housekeeping and transportation services whether it be to the store, hairdresser/barber or a medical appointment
- have a scheduled calendar of events for residents and their families that includes arts and crafts, current events and field trips
- assist with dressing, personal hygiene and medications
- have a resident doctor and/or registered nurse on staff

ADULT DAY CARE

Adult Day Care Centers are designed to provide care and companionship for older adults who need assistance or supervision during the day. One of the main advantages of adult day care is that they offer the relief to family members and caregivers, allowing them to go to work, handle personal business, or just relax while knowing their relative is well cared for and safe. The goals of the programs are to delay or prevent institutionalization by providing alternative care, to enhance self-esteem and to encourage socialization.

There are two types of adult day care: adult social day care and adult day health care. Adult social day care provides social activities, meals, recreation, and some health-related services. Adult day health care offers intensive health, therapeutic, and social services for individuals with serious medical conditions and those at risk of requiring nursing home care.

AGING-IN-PLACE

Aging-in-place refers to you or your loved one's ability to remain in the place where he or she is residing even when their health declines significantly. The term is mostly used in connection with housing options when the ALF extends programs and services to residents who suffer physical or mental impairments, or who may need hospice care, and there by allow the elder to remain living in the ALF and not leave to the skilled nursing facility. The reality is that assisted living generally becomes the elder's home after a period of adjustment, so removing the elder can be a traumatic and deflating experience, especially if dementia is involved. Aging-in-place services in assisted living facilities offer an alternative to nursing homes for those residents whose conditions decline or are nearing end-of-life and who do not wish to be transferred to another facility.

Aging-in-place requires the ALF to manage the resident's care for as long as he or she desires to continue to reside there despite any changes in the resident's physical, cognitive, or emotional condition. Many who move to another facility often suffer setbacks (generally referred to as a "functional decline") as a result of the stress of a move and changes in environment, care, and services, aging-in-place programs can offer an important advantage to residents and families, which is especially true with regards to patients with dementia. Aging-in-place can afford a resident continuity of care and continued support of friends and caregivers at a time when a resident's condition may be very frail.

Assisted living facilities, by regulation, cannot provide skilled nursing services such as wound care (beyond stage 2), intravenous medications, or full lift by two people. Thus, when the patient may have to move from the ALF due to these issues, Hospice may be able to come in to coordinate services under their own license. This will avoid a great deal of confusion and other issues that may happen at the end stages of life. With the assistance and involvement of the facility nursing staff, your local hospice may follow and monitor the resident's condition for as long as necessary.

Key Point to Remember:

- One of the key parts of aging can be socialization. While many people try to stay at home for as long as possible, moving to independent or assisted living can truly be a wonderful experience for most.

- One of the keys to successful aging is adapting to changes that come and making the most of life. Attitude is everything.

CHAPTER 3
HOW TO FIND A GOOD LONG-TERM CARE FACILITY

FINDING GOOD CARE in a good facility can be very time consuming, frustrating and difficult. Sometimes the local facilities will have a good number of Medicare and long-term care beds available, other times it is very difficult to get your loved one into a facility at all. This means that finding a nursing home is not easy under most circumstances and finding a good facility that gives good care can be even more difficult.

One of the first resources people look to is https://www.medicare.gov/nursinghomecompare, which brings up a list of skilled nursing facilities in the local area and provides them a star rating system. Florida has a specific website at http://www.floridahealthfinder.gov/ for both assisted living and nursing home facilities. These are both excellent places to start without having to leave home.

FOUR STEP PROCESS TO FINDING A NURSING HOME

Follow these steps to find the nursing home that meets your needs.

Step 1: Find nursing homes in your area. See below.

Step 2: Compare the quality of the nursing homes you're considering.

Step 3: *Visit the nursing homes you're interested in or have someone visit for you.*

Step 4: *Choose the nursing home that meets your needs.*

STEP 1:
FIND NURSING HOMES IN YOUR AREA.

To learn about the nursing homes in your area:

- Ask people you trust, like your family, friends, or neighbors if they've had personal experience with nursing homes. They may be able to recommend a nursing home to you.
- Ask your doctor if he or she provides care at any local nursing homes. If so, ask your doctor which nursing homes he or she visits so you may continue to see him or her while you're in the nursing home.
- Visit the websites mentioned above.
- Contact your local senior and community activity center.
- If you're in the hospital, ask your social worker about discharge planning as early in your hospital stay as possible. The hospital's staff should be able to help you find a nursing home that meets your needs and help with your transfer when you're ready to be discharged.
- Your elder law attorney may be able to guide you here.

STEP 2:
COMPARE THE QUALITY OF THE NURSING HOMES YOU'RE CONSIDERING.

Compare the care that nursing homes provide to help find the nursing home that meets your needs. Visit Medicare.gov/

nursing home compare to compare the nursing home quality of every Medicare and Medicaid-certified nursing home in the country. Consider the information on Nursing Home Compare carefully. Use it along with other information you gather about nursing homes.

Other ways to find out about nursing home quality, you may want to use a variety of resources when choosing a nursing home:

- Visit the nursing homes you're considering, if possible, or have someone visit for you.
- Ask if they have written information on the quality of care given in local nursing homes. You can also ask for a copy of the full survey or the last complaint investigation report.
- Your elder law attorney may have relationships with good (and bad) local facilities.

Look at survey findings (CMS Form 2567) for the facility, which may be found in the lobby area.

STEP 3:
VISIT THE NURSING HOMES YOU'RE INTERESTED IN OR HAVE SOMEONE VISIT FOR YOU.

Before you visit any nursing homes, consider what's important to you and think about the questions below. Some of these questions ask about rights and protections that are guaranteed to you as a nursing home resident, like being treated in a respectful way.

Other questions ask about preferences that may not be guaranteed, like bringing a pet into a nursing home. Be sure to think about what's important to you before you pick a nursing home.

QUALITY OF LIFE

- Will I be treated in a respectful way?
- How will the nursing home help me participate in social, recreational, religious, or cultural activities that are important to me? Can I decide when I want to participate?
- Do I get to choose what time to get up, go to sleep, or bathe?
- Can I have visitors at any time? Will the nursing home let me see visitors who may come to visit at early or late hours?
- Is transportation provided to community activities?
- Can I bring my pet, or can my pet visit?
- Can I decorate my living space any way I want?
- How will the nursing home make sure I have privacy when I have visitors or personal care services?
- Would I be able to leave the facility for a few hours or days if I choose to do so? Are there procedures for leaving?
- Are there a variety of activities/programming being offered in the facility?

QUALITY OF CARE

- What's a plan of care, and what does it look like?
- Who makes the plan of care, and how do they know what I want, need, or what should be in the plan?

- Will I be included in planning my care?
    — Will my interests and preferences be included in the care plan?
    — Will I be able to change the plan if I feel there's a need?
    — Will I be able to choose which of my family members or friends will be involved in the planning process?
    — Will I get a copy of my care plan?
- Who are the doctors who will care for me? Can I still see my personal doctors? Who will help me arrange transportation if I choose to continue to see my personal doctors and they don't visit the nursing home?
- Who will give me the care I need?
- If a resident has a problem with confusion and wanders, how does the staff handle this type of behavior to protect the residents?
- Does the nursing home's inspection report show quality of care problems (deficiencies)?
- What does the quality information on Nursing Home Compare at Medicare.gov/nursinghomecompare show about how well this nursing home cares for its residents?

AVAILABILITY

- Is a bed available now, or can I add my name to a waiting list? Note: Nursing homes don't have to accept all applications, but they must comply with local, state, and federal civil rights laws that prohibit discrimination.

STAFFING

- Is there enough staff to give me the care I need?

HOW TO FIND A GOOD LONG-TERM FACILITY

- Will I have the same staff people take care of me day to day or do they change?
- Does the nursing home post information about the number of nursing staff, including Certified Nursing Assistants (CNAs)? Are they willing to show me if I ask to see it? (*Note:* Nursing homes are required to post this information.)
- How many residents is a CNA assigned to work with during each shift (day and night) and during meals?
- What type of therapy is available at this facility? Are therapy staff available?
- Is there a social worker available? Can I meet him or her?

(*Note:* Nursing homes must provide medically related social services but if the nursing home has less than 120 beds, it doesn't have to have a full-time social worker on staff.)

FOOD & DINING

- Does the nursing home have food service that I would be happy with?
- Does the nursing home provide a pleasant dining experience?
- Does the staff help residents eat and drink at mealtimes if help is needed?
- What types of meals does the nursing home serve? (Note: Ask the nursing home if you can see a menu.)
- Can I get food and drinks I like at any time? What if I don't like the food that's served?

- Do residents have a choice of food items at each meal? Are there options and substitutes available if I don't like a particular meal?
- Can the nursing home provide for my dietary needs?

If you want to learn more about finding a good long-term care facility for your loved one, please visit https://www.medicare.gov/Pubs/pdf/02174.pdf

Summation: Finding a good long-term care facility can be very difficult. Remember that it is about the patient's care and not the pretty carpets.

CHAPTER 4

LONG-TERM CARE CAN BE VERY EXPENSIVE

LOOKING BACK AT Sally's situation from page 13, Sally has fallen and is getting rehabilitation with Medicare paying at this point. Once Medicare (as discussed in Chapter 10) will not pay for Sally's care, the family is now faced with not only getting good care but also figuring out how to pay for it. This is when the family is shocked into reality – that long-term care is expensive!

In the event Sally were able to go home, in-home care costs can accumulate quickly. Home health care workers generally charge $18-$23/hour in Florida. If full time care is needed to keep you safe at home, in-home care could cost you over $170,000.00 per year. ($20/hour x 24/hours per day x 365 days=$175,200). This means that long-term, full-time, in-home care is not economically feasible for anyone except the wealthy.

The cost for regular assisted living care generally ranges from $2,000 to $7,000 per month in Florida, with an average cost of around $4,000 per month. The reality is that finding a good assisted living facility for your loved one is very difficult due to the size, amenities, quality and care levels offered. While choosing ALFs for your loved one, you may find small "mom and pop" facilities that offer basic care and you may also find large facilities run by national corporations that are very costly.

For those who are too medically fragile for assisted living, a nursing home is the only option. While nursing homes are not always the terrible place some may think, most of us would much rather not live in a nursing home. The costs of long-term care in a nursing home generally range from $8,000 to $10,000 per month in Florida.

With these high long-term care costs, most people will find it essential to preserve as much of their assets as they can for as long as possible. Asset preservation is another consideration to take into account when you are creating your estate plan.

SUMMARY OF LONG-TERM CARE COSTS

To usefully educate a family on how to pay for the long-term care of your client, you need to have a basic knowledge of the cost of long-term care. In 2018, we can generally say that the cost for long-term care in Florida is as follows:

- $8,000-$11,000/month for a semi-private room in a SNF
- $2,000-$6,000/month for assisted living care
- $3,000-$7,000/month for assisted living care in a dementia (secured) unit
- $20/hour for private care from an agency ($175,200/annually at 24/7 care)
- $75/day for adult day care

HOW LONG COULD YOU AFFORD LONG-TERM CARE?

When you or your loved one is looking at not being able to stay at home any longer. Part of the worries include how long your loved one's funds will last and whether the family will need to help pay to keep their loved on in the correct place.

In our example with Sally, our typical client, let's look at her situation again with some of her finances in place:

- Sally is age 93
- Life Expectancy: 3.76 years (Florida Department of Children and Families)
- Income of $2,000 per month from a pension and Social Security
- Assets of $100,000 in bank accounts and CDs

If the family found a good assisted living facility for Sally at the rate of $3,500 per month, Sally would spend approximately $18,000/year (out of pocket) on ALF costs. Based upon Sally's life expectancy, we would expect that her money would last her for the rest of her life, spending some $68,000 out of pocket for her ALF care. This assumes, of course, that Sally will not go downhill further and will not need to stay in the skilled nursing facility.

In the event Sally could not leave the skilled nursing facility because she needs too much care, then Sally's money will deplete very quickly. If long-term care in the nursing home cost $9,000 per month, Sally's funds will last about 14 months, assuming no other costs.

One of the reasons that families get so concerned about funds is that they have the fear of the unknown – what happens when or if you or your loved one's assets are depleted? This is why, of course, good elder law attorneys exist – in order to help you make the right decisions on your loved one's care, placement and how long their funds will last.

Key Point to Remember:

> Long-term care is very expensive and should be planned for as part of your estate plan in order to preserve assets for yourself and for your family.

> If you want to prepare for your future long-term care, you want to look at things before you get sick. Traditionally, you would want to purchase financial products, such as long-term care insurance, in your 60's. More about financial planning with long-term care insurance is discussed in the following chapters.

> When creating your estate plan, ask your attorney if they would recommend you trying to protect your assets. Asset protection for Medicaid purposes is discussed in Chapter 16.

SECTION 2:
WHAT TO KNOW BEFORE YOU NEED LONG-TERM CARE

Chapter 5:
Staying at Home for as Long as Possible

Chapter 6:
Long-Term Care Insurance and You

Chapter 7:
Annuity-Based Long-Term Care and The Pension Protection Act of 2006 by Don Quante

Chapter 8:
Life Insurance/Long-Term Care Strategy by Don Quante

Chapter 9:
Asset-Based Long-Term Care Strategy by Don Quante

Chapter 10:
Understanding Health Insurance: Medicare and HMOs

CHAPTER 5
STAYING AT HOME FOR AS LONG AS POSSIBLE

THE MAJORITY OF us will receive care at home until care or money concerns will not allow us to stay at home any longer. This chapter will discuss some of the concerns about staying home longer, even when it may not be as important as you might think.

DO YOU REALLY WANT TO STAY HOME?

Most of us would much rather stay at home until we die a natural death, but there is the reality that staying home may not be the best thing for us as we age. One practical matter about aging, and one of the most depressing parts about it, is that our friends all start to die and/or have health issues. Thus, your social circle that you once had gets small and smaller as time goes on.

One solution to this is proper socialization as we age. It is easy to overlook the importance of socialization for older adults. Human nature leads us to crave fulfilling relationships with other people. As we age however, life circumstances may push us toward loneliness and isolation unless we take proactive steps to cultivate new relationships. This applies regardless of whether someone lives alone or in an assisted living community. The reality is that receiving our socialization in a long-term care setting, outside of our home, may be better than staying at home at all costs. Consider some of the benefits of socialization for your aging loved one.

SENSE OF PURPOSE AND BELONGING

The combined advantages of active socializing can enhance your loved one's quality of life considerably and add years to their expected lifespan. Moving to assisted living or independent living will allow you or your loved one to make new friends and strengthen existing relationships when they are engaged in activities they love with others who enjoy the same interests. While you may have the ability to stay home does not mean that you should stay home for socialization reasons alone.

INCREASED SELF-CONFIDENCE AND SELF-ESTEEM

Moving to a long-term care facility or having other socialization opportunities such as joining a group of people with the same interests makes life more fun. Those in good health can volunteer or work jobs that can provide a reason to get up and go with a smile. Feeling helpful and needed often makes a huge difference in anyone's life, no matter their age.

IMPROVED HEALTH

Spending time with others in your same age and seeing their similar struggles raises self-confidence. So does keeping up with current news and trends that can occur with increased socialization. Think about how your loved one would feel if he/she was asked to lead a current events group, use a computer, or offer tips on learning the basics of a smartphone. Even still, how proud would they feel if they were asked to teach a group of peers how to play poker, figure out a Sudoku puzzle, or bake a special family recipe. Many of the activities could occur at home or in a long-term care facility.

Anything that boosts self-esteem and self-confidence can contribute to a positive mental outlook, which in turn encourages the release of "good" hormones. These health-promoting chemicals help the body to fight off illness and disease while physically making us feel better. In addition, regular interaction and engagement with peers helps to keep the mind sharp.

TRUE STORY

My 92 year old client was living at home. Her children knew she was getting forgetful and was actually found wondering the streets one night due to confusion. The son did not know what to do as mom did not want to leave the home, like many elders. The son would visit mom every day to make sure she was safe. During the son's visit, mom fell and the son did not have time to catch her. The fall set for a series of health declines where eventually mom had to stay in the nursing home for the rest of her life. If she did not have her son at home with her, my client would have likely been on the floor for more than a day, which would have been an awful experience for her.

FALL RISKS WHILE AT HOME

Did you know that one in three older Americans falls every year? Falls are the leading cause of both fatal and nonfatal injuries for the elderly. Falls can result in hip fractures, broken bones, and head injuries and significant loss of independence. Falls often trigger the onset of a series of growing needs. For those over age 75, fallers are more than four times more likely to be admitted to a skilled nursing facility. A large fall or a series of falls can lead to a hospital stay and time in the rehabilitation facility. And falls, even without a major injury, can cause an older adult to become fearful or depressed, making it difficult for them to stay active.

The good news about falls is that most of them can be prevented. The key is to know where to look. Here are some steps developed by the National Council on Aging (NCOA) to help your older loved one reduce their risk of a fall:

6 STEPS TO REDUCING FALLS (SOURCE: NATIONAL COUNCIL ON AGING)

1. Enlist their support in taking simple steps to stay safe. For example:

   - Ask your older loved one if they're concerned about falling

   - Many older adults recognize that falling is a risk, but they believe it won't happen to them or they won't get hurt—even if they've already fallen in the past

   - A good place to start is by sharing NCOA's Debunking the Myths of Older Adult Falls. If they're concerned about falling, dizziness, or balance, suggest that they discuss it with their health care provider who can assess their risk and suggest programs or services that could help

2. Discuss their current health conditions:
- Find out if your older loved one is experiencing any problems with managing their own health
- Ask whether they are having trouble remembering to take their medications—or are they experiencing side effects?
- Ask if it is getting more difficult for them to do things they used to do easily?
- Also make sure they're taking advantage of all the preventive benefits now offered under Medicare, such as the Annual Wellness visit. Encourage them to speak openly with their health care provider about all of their concerns

3. Ask about their last eye checkup:
- If your older loved one wears glasses or contact lenses, make sure they have a current prescription and they're using the glasses/contacts as advised by their eye doctor
- Remember that using tint-changing lenses can be hazardous when going from bright sun into darkened buildings and homes. A simple strategy is to change glasses upon entry or stop until their lenses adjust
- Bifocals also can be problematic on stairs, so it's important to be cautious. For those already struggling with low vision, consult with a low-vision specialist for ways to make the most of their eyesight

4. Notice if they're holding onto walls, furniture, or someone else when walking or if they appear to have difficulty walking or arising from a chair, because:

- These are all signs that it might be time to see a physical therapist
- A trained physical therapist can help your older loved one improve their balance, strength, and gait through exercise
- They might also suggest a cane or walker—and provide guidance on how to use these aids. Make sure to follow their advice.
- Poorly fit aids actually can increase the risk of falling

5. Talk about their medications:
   - If your older loved one is having a hard time keeping track of medicines or is experiencing side effects, encourage them to discuss their concerns with their doctor and pharmacist
   - Suggest that they have their medications reviewed each time they get a new prescription
   - Some find it useful to use a spread sheet to keep track of medications and schedules. Adding a timed medication dispenser that can be refilled each month by a family member can also promote peace of mind and ensure adherence to the prescribed regime
   - Beware of non-prescription medications that contain sleep aids—including painkillers with "PM" in their names. These can lead to balance issues and dizziness. If your older loved one is having sleeping problems, encourage them to talk to their doctor or pharmacist about safer alternatives.

6. Do a walk-through safety assessment of their home.

There are many simple and inexpensive ways to make a home safer. For professional assistance, consult an Occupational Therapist. Here are some examples:

- **Lighting:** Increase lighting throughout the house, especially at the top and bottom of stairs. Ensure that lighting is readily available when getting up in the middle of the night
- **Stairs:** Make sure there are two secure rails on all stairs
- **Bathrooms:** Install grab bars in the tub/shower and near the toilet. Make sure they're installed where your older loved one would actually use them. For even greater safety, consider using a shower chair and hand-held shower

PERSONAL EMERGENCY RESPONSE SYSTEMS

Staying at home the longer you age means that you will likely need a Personal Emergency Response System (PERS). Also known as a Medical Emergency Response System, these devices let you call for help in an emergency by pushing a button. A PERS has three components: a small radio transmitter, a console connected to your telephone, and an emergency response center that monitors calls.

Transmitters are light-weight, battery-powered devices. You or your loved one can wear one around your neck, on a wrist band, on a belt, or in your pocket. When you need help, you press the transmitter's help button, which sends a signal to the console. The console automatically dials one or more emergency telephone numbers. Most PERS are programmed to telephone an emergency response center. The center will try to find out the nature of your emergency. They also may review your medical history and check who should be notified.

You can purchase, rent, or lease a PERS. Keep in mind that Medicare, Medicaid, and most insurance companies typically don't pay for the equipment, and the few that pay require a doctor's recommendation. Some hospitals and social service agencies may subsidize the device for low-income users. If you buy a PERS, expect to pay an installation fee and a monthly monitoring charge. Rentals are available through national manufacturers, local distributors, hospitals, and social service agencies, and fees often include the monitoring service. Read the contract carefully before you sign, and make note of extra charges, like cancellation fees.

Your local Area Agency on Aging may be able to tell you what systems are available in your area. See if friends, neighbors, or relatives have recommendations. When you have a list of agencies you're considering, check with your local consumer protection agency, state Attorney General, and Better Business Bureau to see if any complaints have been filed against them. Questions you can ask a PERS company include:

- Is the monitoring center open 24/7? What kind of training do staff receive?
- What's the average response time, and who gets alerted?
- Will I be able to use the same system with other response centers if I move? What if I move to another city or state?
- What's your repair policy? What happens if I need a replacement?

- What are the initial costs? What costs are ongoing? What kind of services and features will I get?

Key Point to Remember:

> Staying at home at all costs is generally not the best planning.
> If you or your loved one wants to stay at home, working together to prevent falls and having systems in place for help will be key.

CHAPTER 6
LONG-TERM CARE INSURANCE AND YOU

ONE KEY WAY to provide you protection and peace of mind is to purchase long-term care insurance while you are healthy and a relatively young age. The basic purposes of long-term care insurance are to:

- Prevent the need to spend down your assets in the event you need long-term care;
- Provide you better care at home rather than in a long-term care facility.
- Give you more control over the choice of a long-term care facility.

LONG-TERM CARE INSURANCE OVERVIEW

Long-Term Care Insurance will basically provide daily (dollar-amount limited) funding for a limited long-term period. These funds will help you cover personal and custodial services or help pay for care in home or in long-term care facilities.

Long-term care insurance pays for many services and procedures that medical insurance rarely covers, including skilled, intermediate, and custodial care (i.e., the nursing home).

- Skilled care is daily, planned treatment, usually ordered by a physician, performed by nurses or physical therapists, and targeted to help you recover from a serious injury or illness.

- Intermediate care follows skilled care protocols, but is provided less frequently.
- Custodial care is not focused on health improvement; it merely provides assistance with daily activities. Custodial care includes anything from in-home care provided two or three times weekly to 24-hour nursing home care.

If you want to protect your estate from the high cost of long-term care, consider long-term care insurance—but it is expensive: It is estimated that only one in five couples can afford to purchase long-term care insurance. The reasons for this vary, but it is generally thought that most people have other insurance and investment needs (i.e., retirement, disability, health) that come before the need to purchase long-term care insurance.

The limited number of people who should even purchase long-term care insurance can generally be categorized as those who:

- Need long-term care insurance and can afford it; and
- Qualify for long-term care insurance due to health reasons.

QUESTION #1
CAN YOU AFFORD LONG-TERM CARE INSURANCE?

The general rule is that you should purchase long-term care insurance if your income allows it, if you have assets to protect, and if long-term care costs would significantly impact those assets and prove to be a hardship on your family.

More specifically, people buy long-term care policies so that, should they need long term care, they will:

1. Have the funds to select and purchase the care they want and need;

2. Be able to maintain and protect the assets they have accumulated over their lifetimes if their savings are substantial;

3. Not be required to "spend down" their assets in order to access Medicaid if their savings are more modest.

Whether to buy long-term care insurance and how much to buy are questions with no clear answers. Those with few assets have other, more pressing, needs than purchasing long-term care insurance, and their "spend down" will be quick. The wealthy—those with liquid assets exceeding $2,000,000—can generally be self-insured since, percentage-wise, the financial impact will be minimal and their money is often working, even when they are not. Some wealthy individuals may have specific reasons for purchasing long-term care insurance which are outside of the scope of our discussion here. As a general rule, people with financial assets over $200,000 (bank accounts, etc.) should at least investigate long-term care policies.

The cost of a long-term care policy will depend on:

- The age when the policy is purchased

- The individual's health when the policy is purchased (certain health conditions will result in higher premiums; others with pre-existing conditions, where the insurance company considers the risk too great, will not be able to purchase policies)
- The maximum daily amount the policy will pay
- The maximum number of days (years) the policy will pay
- The lifetime maximum amount the policy will pay (maximum daily amount times the number of days)
- Optional benefits chosen; e.g., benefits that increase with inflation

AARP has estimated that a single person needs to have an annual retirement income of $25,000 to $35,000 and a couple will need $35,000 to $50,000. Companies may raise their long-term care premiums as years go by and the policy holder gets older. These increases may come at a time where income decreases, which is also at a time where the likelihood of needing long-term care markedly increases. Whatever policy you decide to get, be aware of the company's history as far as raising premium rates and have a plan in place to be able to continue to pay your premiums. You need be able to afford possible rate increases and not be forced to drop the policy.

QUESTION #2
DO YOU QUALIFY FOR LONG-TERM CARE INSURANCE?

It is common sense that the younger you are, the cheaper your long-term care insurance policy will be, and that the price will increase as you age. A (generally) good policy paying out

$145/day may start out at $1,500/year at age fifty (50) and will generally increase to $3,400/year by age sixty-five (65).

Long-term care services are not just for older people. An estimated twenty percent of long-term care patients are under age 65, receiving long-term care due to accidents or debilitating illnesses. Yet, at any given age in younger years, long-term care is the exception rather than the rule, and the outcome can often, thankfully, be a return to health and productivity. For the elderly, long-term care is more a matter of careful and compassionate management of an individual's health in an attempt to maintain as much capacity as possible, and provide for the patient a measure of dignity, comfort, and enjoyment of life.

Aside from the risk of needing long-term care at a younger age than you might expect and the increased cost for coverage as you get older, a more critical problem with waiting to purchase a policy is that you may become uninsurable due to the discovery of a previously undiagnosed and/or new development of a health condition. Insurance experts estimate that one in five persons at age sixty (60) already do not qualify for long-term care insurance due to health issues.

WHAT SHOULD I CONSIDER IF I WANT TO BUY LONG-TERM CARE INSURANCE?

MANY FACTORS CONTRIBUTE to your need for and the cost of long-term care insurance. These include:

- Your age and health. The younger you are, the more likely you are healthy, which decreases your premium.
- Your family history of chronic illness or dementia.

- Your marital status – single people generally have more of a need for long-term care insurance.
- Your own support system with local family who can take you into their homes or move in and live with you, for instance.
- Your gender. Women more likely need long-term care insurance due to their relative longevity.
- Your income and assets. Can you afford long-term care insurance without sacrificing your standard of living?
- The company's reputation, underwriting requirements, and pricing.

PURCHASING LONG-TERM CARE INSURANCE

Florida Statutes established a qualified Long-Term Care Insurance Partnership Program to:

1. Provide incentives for individuals to obtain or maintain long-term care insurance;
2. Provide a mechanism for individuals to qualify for long-term care Medicaid coverage without first being required to substantially deplete his or her assets; and
3. Reduce an individual's total countable assets by an amount equal to the insurance benefit payments made to or on behalf of the individual.

The nonprofit organization Life Happens has a helpful website which describes the different types of insurance and their uses. www.lifehappens.org. The site has calculators to determine how much life insurance and disability insurance you need and will provide your Human Life Value, an estimate of your future earnings and the financial loss your family would suffer should you die today. The site also has an interactive page where you can select the type of insurance you need and enter your city or zip code to find agents who sell that type of insurance. However, the site does not include A.M. Best ratings.

A.M. Best is a U.S.-based rating agency which evaluates and reports on the financial strength of insurance companies. These ratings measure insurance companies' ability to pay claims. When you purchase insurance, you want to be sure the company will be able to pay you when the money is due.

The top rated companies are "aaa" rated, with an expected "exceptional ability to meet the terms of the obligation; "aa" companies have a superior ability; and "a" companies, excellent. From there on, it's downhill. A "bbb" company is "good," but the company is more susceptible to economic changes; a "bb" company is "fair," with more risk involved; a "b" company is considered to be marginal; and "ccc," "cc," and "c" are weak, very weak, and poor. Unlike school, "c" is not a passing grade.

If you want to make a wise insurance investment, make sure the company you choose has at *least* an A.M. Best rating of "a" better. If your agent does not supply that information (he or she absolutely should) Google the "name of the insurance company" you are considering and "A.M. Best rating" and you will get the information you need.

THE RECENT DECLINE OF LONG-TERM CARE INSURANCE

Traditional long-term care insurance (LTCI) is becoming less and less popular in recent years. Traditional policy sales have fallen over 60 percent since 2012 according to LIMRA, an insurance industry research and consulting group. In 2016, only 91,000 traditional long-term care policies were sold.

One aspect is that LTCI companies have lost a great deal of money on their policies. The insurance companies failed to accurately predict the number of claimants and have had to raise rates. Rate increases approved by regulators have averaged more than 20 percent annually in recent years and many carriers have stopped writing new policies.

One main objection to traditional LTCI is that people object to the "use it or lose it" policy aspects. You could pay premiums for many years and you never used the policy before your death. The feeling is that the policy premiums would just go down the drain, having never been used.

Importantly, there are new combination life insurance and annuity products that contain long-term care insurance riders. These combination financial products with long-term care insurance are becoming much more popular that will be discussed in the next chapters.

Key Points to Remember:

- Consider purchasing long-term care insurance in your 50's or 60's if you have the financial means.
- Some (i.e., less coverage) long-term care insurance is likely better than no long-term care insurance.
- Finding long-term care insurance is not easy – take your time and work with a representative who works with multiple insurance companies and whom you trust.
- The following chapters will contain more information about asset based long-term care insurance products.

CHAPTER 7

ANNUITY-BASED LONG-TERM CARE AND THE PENSION PROTECTION ACT OF 2006 BY DON QUANTE

ON AUGUST 17, 2006, the President signed into law The Pension Protection Act of 2006 (the "Act"). Individuals owning annuity contracts can now have long-term care riders with special tax advantages. The Act allows the cash value of annuity contracts to be used to pay premiums on long-term care contracts. The payment of premiums in this manner will reduce the cost basis of the annuity contract. In addition, the Act allows annuity contracts without long-term care riders to be exchanged for contracts with such a rider in a tax-free transfer under Section 1035 of the Internal Revenue Code of 1986, as amended ("IRC"). This provision may prove beneficial to individuals who own annuities with a low cost basis and those who are not in the best of health. The cash value of the annuity can be used to purchase long-term care insurance. This provision is effective for exchanges which take place after 2009.

An example of how an annuity-based long-term care plan could help someone is illustrated in Exhibit 7.1. For this example, we will call our client Bob, age 70, and recently widowed. His children lived out of town and they were very concerned about what would happen if dad needed some additional care in the future. Since Bob had some health concerns and was recently diagnosed with diabetes, along with a history of heart disease, he was not a good candidate for traditional long-term care insurance. However, by taking advantage of an annuity based long-term care strategy that takes advantage of the Pen- sion Protection Act, Bob could likely be insured. By taking his

$140,000 fixed annuity with a cost basis of only 40,000 (i.e. the amount he actually deposited) and using the IRS 1035 tax-free exchange from his existing fixed annuity to a new annuity that complied with the rules laid out in the Pension Protection Act, Bob's $140,000 fixed annuity could continue to earn interest. However, if he needed long-term care to pay for home care, assisted living, or skilled care he now had a long-term care pool of money equal to $420,000. (See exhibit 7.1.)*

Exhibit 7.1

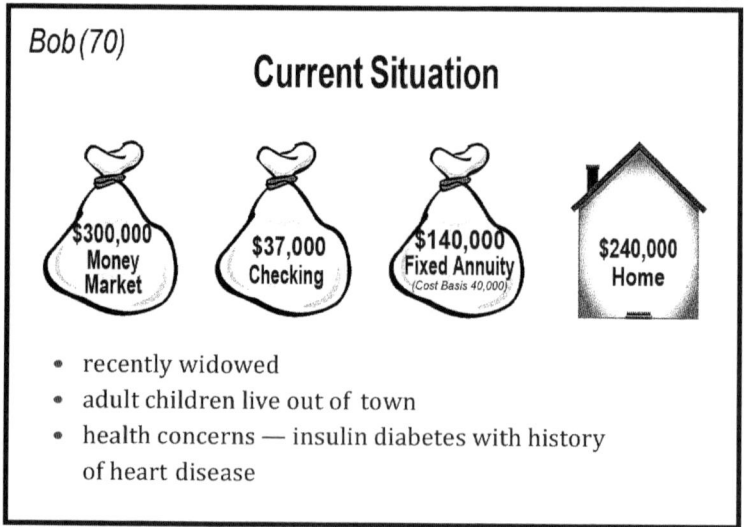

Bob (70)

Current Situation

$300,000 Money Market $37,000 Checking $140,000 Fixed Annuity (Cost Basis 40,000) $240,000 Home

- recently widowed
- adult children live out of town
- health concerns — insulin diabetes with history of heart disease

---

* Not all products are available in all states.

Bob (70)
Proposed

$140,000 Fixed Annuity → Combo LTC Annuity → $420,000 LTC Pool

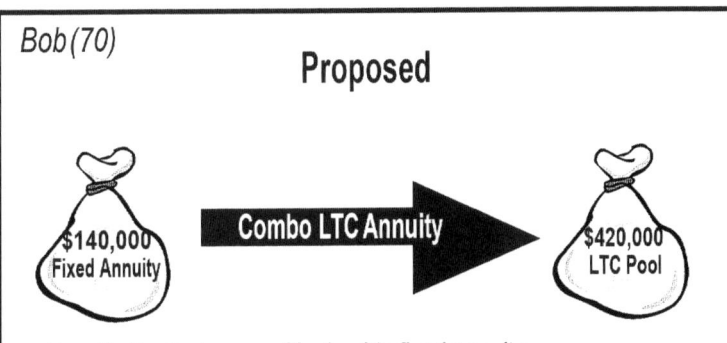

Hypothetically, by repositioning his fixed annuity...

- Bob retains his $140,000 in cash value plus an additional $280,000 for a total of $420,000 for long-term care.
- His benefits may be used for home care, assisted living, and skilled care.
- He pays no annual premiums.
- As his annuity grows, so does his LTC! (Assuming he does not use his LTC benefit.)

CHAPTER 8

LIFE INSURANCE/LONG-TERM CARE STRATEGY
BY DON QUANTE

UNTIL RECENTLY, THE thought of using a life insurance policy to pay for long-term care expenses was unthinkable. However, with the first baby boomers reaching the milestone of age 65 on January 1 of 2011, the insurance companies have begun offering long-term care coverage as a rider on term life policies as well as whole life and universal life policies.

The basic concept is that the insurance company will allow the insured to accelerate the death benefit of the policy if the insured is unable to perform two of the six activities of daily living (eating, dressing, bathing, transferring, toileting or continence) or if the insured is cognitively impaired. The most attractive feature of this type of plan is the ability of the insured to use the money to pay for home healthcare, assisted living, or skilled care. The policy will even allow you to pick who your caregiver is—including family members. This strategy is illustrated in Exhibit 8.1

---

* Not all products are available in all states.

LIFE INSURANCE/LONG-TERM CARE STRATEGY BY DON QUANTE

Exhibit 8.1

Sue (45)

Current Situation

- Sue is a single mom and has children going to college.
- She currently has a 20-year term and is in year 18.
- Sue feels strongly about never wanting to go to a nursing home.
- She would like to buy long-term care insurance, but does not feel like she can afford the premiums.

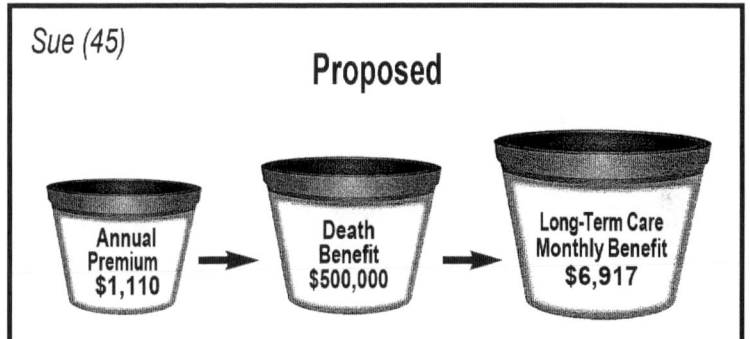

Sue (45)

Proposed

Annual Premium $1,110 → Death Benefit $500,000 → Long-Term Care Monthly Benefit $6,917

Sue's Solution—30 Year Term with LTC Rider*

- provide for an LTC Program by replacing existing term insurance
- choice of where she wants to receive her care
- choice of caregiver (even family members)
- provide tax-free death benefit to her children if she does not need long-term care—$500,000

CHAPTER 9
ASSET-BASED LONG-TERM CARE STRATEGY BY DON QUANTE

"Legacy assets" are those assets in a retiree's portfolio that do not support their lifestyle, but are available in case of some serious emergency (rainy day money!).

These assets, if (hopefully) never needed, will probably pass to the clients' children, church, or charity after they die. The one most significant risk to those assets is the need to pay for long-term care.

Many people in this situation resist the idea of conventional long-term care insurance, not wanting to admit that they might need it, and taking the position that they can pay for any care out of pocket. They are choosing to "self insure." For these individuals, the ideal planning approach would be to "invest" some of their legacy assets in such a way that the assets can be worth as much as possible whenever they may be needed to pay for care…in the home, assisted-living facility, or nursing home. If not needed, the money would then pass to the intended heirs, with no "use it, or lose it" issues as with conventional long-term care insurance.

To employ this strategy, money is transferred from its current location (bank account, fixed annuity, etc.) into a specially-designed life insurance policy with riders that prepay the death benefit, and additionally to reimburse the insured for the incurred costs of long-term care. Depending on age, sex and health status, the money paid into one of these policies may be worth twice as much if the insured dies without ever needing to use it. Also, if needed for convalescent care, the insured can receive up to five times the amount of money deposited into the contract. Any money not used for that purpose would then pass to the heirs at death (See Exhibit 9.1).*

While invested in the insurance policy, the client's money is safe and available for any other reason at any time. There is usually a money-back guarantee that assures that the policy- holder will always have access to the funds. Rather than a typical "purchase" of insurance, the transaction is more like "moving money from one account to another"…a cash value account that provides the same "savings" features as the bank, bond, or annuity from which it came.

Because the actual cost of long-term care is so great (potentially $70,000 per year or more) and the average need exceeds 2 years, these policies are usually purchased with a rider that extends the long-term care benefits after the death benefit has been exhausted. These riders effectively double or triple the benefit so that in the example (See Exhibit 9.1), a $50,000 pre- mium deposit can provide as much as $250,000 in total long-term care benefits, providing as much as six years worth of protection.

This approach is ideal for those individuals who reject the idea of purchasing conventional, annual-premium long-term care insurance policies and take the position that if they ever need long-term convalescent care, they will pay for it using their own assets.

* Not all products are available in all states.

Exhibit 9.1

Mary's Hypothetical Situation
Proposed Strategy

- It provides LTC by repositioning assets.
- Mary can choose where to receive care with income tax-free LTC benefits.
- Income tax-free death benefit for children if she does not need long-term care.
- 100% of the premium is returned (within the timeframe and conditions allowed in the policy) if Mary changes her mind or finds a better solution.
- LTC benefits are guaranteed without worries of future premium increases.

Note: The death benefit on these policies typically declines dollar for dollar based on the amount of LTC benefit needed. If Mary needs a $20,000 LTC withdrawal, her death benefit would be reduced by $20,000 to $80,000.

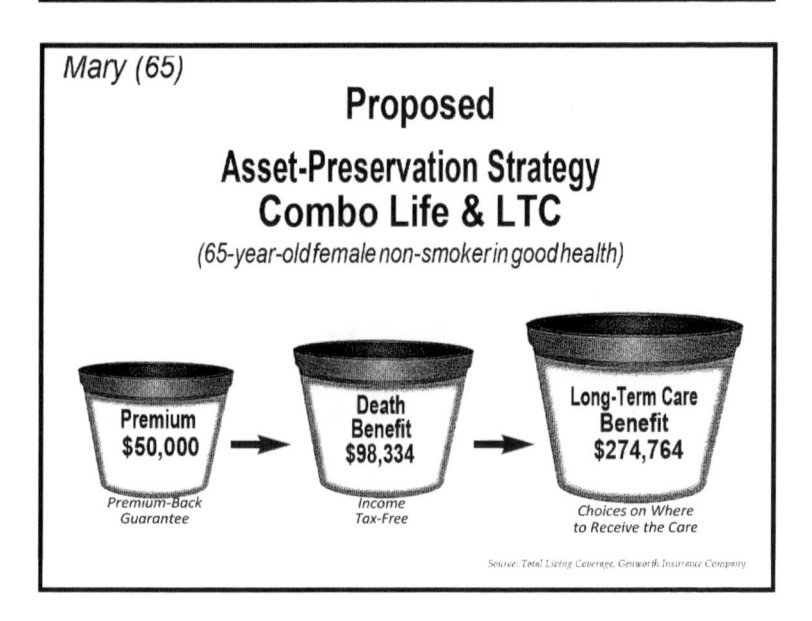

Mary (65)

Proposed
Asset-Preservation Strategy
Combo Life & LTC

(65-year-old female non-smoker in good health)

Premium $50,000	→	Death Benefit $98,334	→	Long-Term Care Benefit $274,764
Premium-Back Guarantee		Income Tax-Free		Choices on Where to Receive the Care

Source: Total Living Coverage, Genworth Insurance Company

For individuals who do not, for whatever reason, want to own any life insurance, there is an alternative. Since the objective is to leverage up the individual's assets if long-term care is needed, some insurance companies are now offering fixed index annuities with guaranteed income riders that double should the individual enter a nursing home (See Exhibit 9.2). Finally, of all the contingencies faced in retirement, long- term care is probably the most difficult and perhaps the most costly… financially as well as emotionally. These asset-based long-term care strategies allow wise consumers to manage their money, and to provide significantly for such a possibility without committing large annual insurance premiums to something they sincerely hope will never be needed. Since the money to do this must reside somewhere, these asset-based long-term care products provide a safe and financially rewarding option.

Exhibit 9.2

Income Preferred Series Calculator

Year Issue	Attained Age	Income Base	Withdrawal Percentage	Withdrawal Payment	Enhanced Withdrawal Payment
0	75	$354,000	n/a	n/a	n/a
1	76	$354,000	5.90%	$20,886	n/a
2	77	$354,000	6.00%	$21,240	n/a
3	78	$362,385	6.00%	$21,743	$43,486
4	79	$385,940	6.00%	$23,156	$46,313
5	80	$411,026	6.00%	$24,662	$49,323
6	81	$437,743	6.00%	$26,265	$52,529
7	82	$466,196	6.00%	$27,972	$55,944
8	83	$496,499	6.00%	$29,790	$59,580
9	84	$528,771	6.00%	$31,726	$63,453
10	85	$563,141	6.00%	$33,788	$67,577
11	86	$599,745	6.00%	$35,985	$71,969
12	87	$638,729	6.00%	$38,324	$76,647
13	88	$680,246	6.00%	$40,815	$81,630
14	89	$724,462	6.00%	$43,468	$86,935
15	90	$771,552	6.00%	$46,293	$92,586
16	91	$821,703	6.00%	$49,302	$98,604
17	92	$875,114	6.00%	$52,507	$105,014
18	93	$931,996	6.00%	$55,920	$111,840
19	94	$992,576	6.00%	$59,555	$119,109
20	95	$1,057,094	6.00%	$63,426	$126,851

* Not all products are available in all states.

Product: Fixed Index Annuity*
Initial Premium: $300,000 (includes any applicable bonus)
Issue Age: 75
Years to Defer: 10
Withdrawal Attained Age: 85
Joint Annuitant: No
Mode of Withdrawal: Annual

The printouts and results displayed by this calculator are approved for consumer use. Please note the actual use and inputting of values are only for appointed LTC producers. The assumptions used in this illustration are guaranteed based on the assumptions you provide in the calculation. The use of alternative premium, age, product, deferral years, and joint life assumptions may produce significantly different results.

66

CHAPTER 10

UNDERSTANDING HEALTH INSURANCE: MEDICARE AND HMOS

MEDICARE AND REHABILITATION are a very common component to dealing with an aging loved. In our scenario with Sally, she is in the SNF and receiving rehab. One of the largest questions we have is how long her Medicare will last and what are our choices as part of the process. We can easily say that dealing with Medicare and HMOs are one of the most difficult parts of dealing with an aging loved one, which typically happens in a crisis type scenario.

One of the most important things to know is that Medicare does not pay for long-term care in a nursing home or assisted living facility. Medicare only covers medically necessary care and focuses on medical acute care, such as doctor visits, drugs, and hospital stays. Medicare coverage also focuses on short-term services for conditions that are expected to improve, such as physical therapy to help you regain your function after a fall or stroke.

ELIGIBILITY

Medicare pays for health care for people age 65 years and older, people under age 65 with certain disabilities, and people of all ages with end-stage renal disease (permanent kidney failure that requires dialysis or a kidney transplant). Paying into the system during your working years gives you access to Medicare benefits as you get older or in the event you become disabled.

LONG-TERM CARE SERVICES – SKILLED NURSING AND MEDICARE

Medicare does not pay the largest part of long-term care services or personal care—such as help with bathing, or for supervision often called custodial care. Medicare will help pay for a short stay in a skilled nursing facility, for hospice care, or for home health care if you meet the following conditions:

- You have had a recent prior hospital stay of at least three days (three full nights)
- You are admitted to a Medicare-certified nursing facility within 30 days of your prior hospital stay
- You need skilled care, such as skilled nursing services, physical therapy, or other types of therapy

If you meet all these conditions, Medicare will pay for some of your costs for up to 100 days. For the first 20 days, Medicare pays 100 percent of your costs. For days 21 through 100, you pay your own expenses up to $167.50 per day (as of 2018), and Medicare pays any balance. You pay 100 percent of costs for each day you stay in a skilled nursing facility after day 100.

LONG-TERM CARE SERVICES – HOME AND OTHER CARE SERVICES

In addition to skilled nursing facility services, Medicare pays for the following services for a limited time when your doctor says they are medically necessary to treat an illness or injury:

- Part-time or intermittent skilled nursing care
- Physical therapy, occupational therapy, and speech-language pathology that your doctor orders that a Medicare-certified home health agency provides for a limited number of days only
- Medical social services to help cope with the social, psychological, cultural, and medical issues that result from an illness. This may include help accessing services and follow-up care, explaining how to use health care and other resources, and help understanding your disease
- Medical supplies and durable medical equipment such as wheelchairs, hospital beds, oxygen, and walkers. For durable medical equipment, you pay 20 percent of the Medicare approved amount

There is no limitation how long you can receive any of these services as long as they're main medically necessary and your doctor reorders them every 60 days.

MEDICARE, MEDIGAP AND HMOS

Health insurance for our aging population generally has three basic options, listed as follows:

a. Medicare (without supplement): Here, you have government provided Medicare but you do not have any insurance to pick up the Medicare co-pays. Medicare is a wonderful health insurance but the co-pays can get expensive, especially at end-of-life or in dealing with the skilled nursing facility/rehabilitation.

b. Medicare (with supplement): This option has Medicare and also has a policy, commonly known as "Medi-Gap") to pick up the difference in Medicare co-pays. You must pay for this out of your own pocket but the cost is typically well worth it, especially in times of healthcare crisis. Policies are classified based upon their required options and have a corresponding letter. The plans are A, B, C, D, E, F (high deductible), G, K, L, M and M. The policy costs generally range from $150-$500/month.

Importantly, not all Medi-Gap plans are created equally. In the elder law world, it is very important that a client purchase a gap policy, recommend that it have Skilled Nursing coverage.

c. Medicare Part C: HMO or PPO (Medicare Replacement): A Medicare Advantage Plan (such as an HMO or PPO) is another health insurance choice. Medicare Advantage Plans, sometimes called "Part C," are offered by private companies approved by Medicare. These plans provide all of your Part A (Hospital Insurance) and Part B (Medical Insurance) coverage. Medicare Advantage Plans may offer extra coverage, such as vision, hearing, dental, and/or health and wellness programs. Most include Medicare prescription drug coverage (Part D).

Medicare pays a fixed amount for your care every month to the companies offering Medicare Advantage Plans. While each company must follow rules set by Medicare, each provider can charge different out-of-pocket costs and have different rules for how you get services (like whether the client needs a referral to see a specialist or if have to go to only doctors, facilities, or suppliers that belong to the plan for non-emergency or non-urgent care).

MEDICARE REPLACEMENTS (HMOS AND PPOS) AND LONG-TERM CARE

Statutorily, Medicare Part C provides the same coverage as straight Medicare but, in practice, Medicare offers more generous rehabilitation benefits than Medicare Replacement plans. Each Medicare replacement plan (Part C) has their own rules for skilled nursing (rehab) discharge and the copays that attend each. Disenrolling from the Part C plan is only allowed under certain circumstances or at certain times of the year. Annually, disenrollment (or changing HMOs) is allowed from October through December.

> ### TRUE STORY:
> We had an elder client in rehab who could not walk and was bedbound. After only two weeks in rehab, and nowhere near as strong as she should be, the HMO discharged her home. Our client could not take care of herself in the least but the HMO insisted that she was safe to go home. At home, our client was so sick we admitted her back to the hospital where she spent 18 more days receiving care. This is just one of many examples of how regular Medicare is much better than Medicare replacement policies when you are sick.

DISCHARGE PLANNING FROM THE SKILLED NURSING FACILITY

When the elder is done receiving skilled nursing rehabilitation, our clients are generally lost on where to go and what to. Can the client go home? Assisted living? Should they stay in the nursing home under custodial long-term care? The SNF should have been prepping the patient (and family) on discharge plans:

- A facility must provide sufficient preparation and orientation to residents to ensure safe and orderly transfer or discharge from the facility.

- Resident records should contain a final resident discharge summary which addresses the resident's post-discharge needs.

- Facilities are to develop a post-discharge plan of care, developed with the participation of the resident and his or her family, which will assist the resident to adjust to his or her new living environment. This applies to discharges to a private residence, to another nursing facility, or to another type of residential facility such as board and care or nursing facilities.

- Post-discharge plan of care means the discharge planning process, which includes assessing continuing care needs and developing a plan designed to ensure the individual's needs will be met after discharge from the facility into the community.

MEDICARE PART B COVERAGE AND LONG-TERM CARE

Medicare Part B helps cover medically-necessary services like doctors' services, outpatient care, durable medical equipment, home health services, and other medical services. Part B also covers some preventive services. In 2018, Medicare Part B costs $130.00/month, which is deducted from your Social Security. This cost may actually rise now based upon the elder's income.

Medicare covers medically-necessary part-time or intermittent skilled nursing care, and/or physical therapy, speech-language pathology services, and/or services for people with a continuing need for occupational therapy. A doctor enrolled in Medicare, or certain health care providers who work with the doctor, must see you face-to-face before the doctor can certify that you need home health services. That doctor must order your care, and a Medicare certified home health agency must provide it.

Home health services may also include medical social services, part-time or intermittent home health aide services, durable medical equipment, and medical supplies for use at home. You must be homebound, which means leaving home is a major effort. You pay nothing for covered home health services.

As mentioned, Medicare and Medicare replacement do not pay for long-term care. They can, at best, provide options for the elder getting stronger while the next placement options are considered.

MEDICARE PART D DRUG COVERAGE

Changing Medicare/Medicare Replacement plans

You are only able to change your Medicare and replacement policies every year in the applicable period, generally October to December. There are, however, some special circumstances where you are able to change from a Medicare replacement plan (Medicare Part C), which is likely needed in the event you or your loved one is receiving rehab. Here, if you just moved into, currently live in, or just moved out of an institution (like a skilled nursing facility or long-term care hospital), you can:

- Join a Medicare Advantage Plan or Medicare Prescription Drug Plan.
- Switch from your current plan to another Medicare Advantage Plan or Medicare Prescription Drug Plan.
- Drop your Medicare Advantage Plan and return to Original Medicare.
- Drop your Medicare prescription drug coverage.

Changing plans in the middle of your rehabilitation may be necessary or advantageous in certain situations. Knowing when and why you would do this is one of the most important aspects of receiving good care in the event you have a catastrophic downturn in health.

Key Points to Remember:

› Medicare with a supplement is generally preferable to a Medicare replacement plan as you age.

› Medicare is generally more lenient in providing rehabilitation services than Medicare replacement plans.

› Medicare replacement plans are likely best for health seniors, those with "silver sneakers," or those with limited income and assets. If you can afford a Medigap policy, this is much better as you age.

› Go to www.Floridashine.org to get unbiased advice on your Medicare/HMO policies.

SECTION 3

GOVERNMENT BENEFITS AND LONG-TERM CARE

Chapter 11
Medicaid and Long-Term Care

Chapter 12
Veterans Benefits and Long-Term Care

Chapter 13
Common Questions and Answers on Medicaid and VA Benefits

CHAPTER 11

MEDICAID AND LONG-TERM CARE

LONG-TERM CARE CAN be very expensive, but the U.S. government offers benefits that can help pay for long-term care in certain situations. While not for every person, Medicaid may help an elder's money last longer, better provide for his or her care, and still allow the elder to leave an inheritance to family.

Medicaid and other government programs are difficult to understand due to the volume and complexity of their many rules, regulations, and practices. We frequently see caregivers receiving conflicting and inaccurate information—often from the governmental entities administering the programs!—at what can be a particularly trying and stressful time in their lives. The following outlines the general guidelines for Medicaid and long-term care.

WHAT IS MEDICAID?

Medicaid is a Federal program, funded from both state and federal dollars, which assists the needy who are unable to cope with both normal (which are already exorbitant) and extraordinary health care costs. Medicaid dollars reimburse health care providers all across the country and cover a wide range of services.

Florida runs its Medicaid program under guidelines provided by the federal government and administers it through the

Department of Children and Families ("DCF"). Applications for Medicaid benefits are made at the DCF.

In working with the elderly, the offices of DeLoach & Hofstra, P.A. facilitate access to Medicaid programs, in particular, those that help pay for nursing home, assisted living facility, or in-home care.

WHY WOULD I NEED MEDICAID?

You will hopefully never need Medicaid, but it can be useful in the event you need to stay long-term at a nursing home or assisted living facility, which can be *very* expensive.

MEDICARE VS. MEDICAID

Medicaid and Medicare are completely different government programs. Medicare was created to subsidize doctor visits, diagnostic and treatment procedures, hospital care, and other related medical purposes for people who are over age 65 or disabled. Medicaid is a "needs-based" system with strict financial requirements. Both Medicaid and Medicare will pay for care in a skilled nursing facility for qualified patients. Medicare coverage includes "skilled" nursing care if the patient is in the hospital for three (3) full days before he or she is transferred into skilled care. Medicare pays the entire cost of care for the first twenty (20) days as long as the patient is generally improving or is responding to therapy. For the next eighty (80) days, the patient bears responsibility for a co-payment of $167.50/day (2018) unless he or she has a Medicare supplemental policy.

Medicare coverage can be terminated at any time if the individual's medical condition does not improve. This means, if a patient is receiving care in a skilled nursing facility, and upon evaluation, is not improving, Medicare STOPS paying, and the patient becomes responsible for any costs incurred thereafter. In our experience, most patients do not receive the full one-hundred (100) days of Medicare benefits. Once Medicare will not pay for your nursing home stay, then you have three (3) options:

1. Stay in the nursing home under long-term care and pay the costs out of your pocket (typically about $280/day);
2. Move to assisted living, which is less expensive. You will receive some level of assistance with the your daily tasks; or
3. Move home.

If you are a member of an HMO instead of Medicare (i.e., using a Medicare replacement, generally known as Medicare Part C), you will need to review the HMO's cost schedule, which has slight variations of the 20/80 rule for therapy in the skilled nursing facility. We generally recommend using traditional Medicare with a gap policy instead of an HMO for a number of reasons, if you can afford it. The primary reason is that traditional Medicare give you more control over your medical care.

With traditional Medicare, you can find out the names of doctors your friends and family recommend, research their records online to make sure they do not have malpractice claims, sanctions, or board actions against them (www.healthgrades.com), and select the physicians and specialists you want to see. If the doctor is outside your "network," you may pay more . . . and some services might not be covered—but you will be permitted to see the out-of-network doctor, and there will be some degree of coverage. You will have greater latitude in selecting the doctors who can best meet your needs–when you need them.

For instance, you might know that a certain medical problem runs in your family. With traditional Medicare, you could make an appointment with a specialist of your choice who treats that condition. . . without first having to go to a primary care doctor to get a referral for a specialist who might or might not be your first choice.

With an HMO, your primary doctor coordinates your healthcare and refers you to specialists. Except in emergencies, if you do not have a referral from your primary doctor to a specialist, Medicare will not pay for the specialist's services. Overall, doctors in HMOs and those who take traditional Medicare are probably equal in skill. But if you are in an HMO and don't like the specialist, you will have to go back to your primary doctor for another referral. If you cannot find an acceptable specialist in-network, you're stuck.

FLORIDA'S MEDICAID ELIGIBILITY REQUIREMENTS

An applicant is not eligible for Florida Medicaid unless he or she meets the asset and income limitations which follow: The applicant must be:

- At least 65 years of age or disabled;
- A United States citizen or a "qualified" alien;
- A Florida resident;

- Income requirement: Gross monthly income must not exceed $2,250/month (2018); and
- Asset requirement: Countable assets for a single person must not exceed $2,000. Assets for a married couple allow the Community Spouse (the spouse not in long-term care) to have around $123,600 (2018) in countable assets.

However, we need to define what "counts" as far as income and assets.

FINANCIAL REQUIREMENTS

Medicaid long-term care benefits are only available to those individuals or couples who meet a complex list of requirements. There are many rules and exceptions that can drastically affect planning. Financial requirements are divided into two separate and distinct categories: income and assets. These two particular requirements rarely interact with each other.

INCOME AND MEDICAID

The applicant's *gross* monthly available income must not exceed $2,250/month (2018). Gross income is not the same as taxable income—Social Security taxes, Medicare Part B premiums, and employee portion of health insurance premiums, are not deducted from gross income!

If the applicant's income exceeds the designated limit, a Qualified Income Trust (QIT) *must* be created and funded to facilitate Medicaid eligibility. This is one reason why a good, current durable power of attorney is necessary as you age.

The income of the spouse staying at home (the "community spouse") is *not* included in determining benefits for the applicant. He or she can have unlimited income. However, if the community spouse's gross income is below a certain level, the community spouse may divert some of the applicant's income for his or her own financial needs. This is known as the *spousal diversion,* which is described as follows.

SPOUSAL INCOME AND MEDICAID

When a single person is in the nursing home on Medicaid, the income and asset rules are fairly straightforward. Find the applicant's gross income, subtract $105 for the personal needs allowance and pay the remainder to the nursing home as part of the patient's responsibility. Income can be a little more complicated when there is a spouse at home.

Rather than requiring a couple to reduce their joint income to poverty level, Florida law permits the community spouse (the spouse at home) to maintain a higher income for self-support if his or her income falls below the minimum monthly maintenance needs allowance (MMMNA). In 2018, for example, Florida allows the community spouse to keep at least $2,058 in monthly income, or up to $3,090 in certain cases as discussed below. First, any income the community spouse receives in his or her own name—Social Security, pension, or dividend income, for example—may be retained fully by the community spouse. Very importantly, no portion of the community spouse's own income is required to be assigned to Medicaid or diverted to cover the cost of care for the institutionalized spouse. As a result, the community spouse's income could exceed the allowed minimum of $2,058. In fact, the community spouse's income can be unlimited. It is only the community spouse's assets that affect the institutionalized spouse's Medicaid.

If, however, the minimum allowance of $2,058/month cannot be met by the community spouse's income alone, Florida allows the institutionalized spouse to divert income to the community spouse to close the gap. This situation may occur, for example, when a husband with greater income is the institutionalized spouse and a wife with a smaller income is the community spouse. In such cases, income that is paid to the institutionalized spouse (such as Social Security and pension income, for example) may be diverted to and retained by the community spouse to assist with his or her basic income needs. The transfer of income from the institutionalized spouse to the community spouse is referred to as the spousal diversion. Calculating income can be confusing but remember that the government is not trying to impoverish the spouse at home and take away all of his or her income. Legal policy is that the government wants to provide a minimum level of support to the community spouse.

EXAMPLE OF THE COMMUNITY SPOUSE INCOME DIVERSION

For example, assume that Sharon and Randy are a senior couple, living in Florida on Randy's monthly $500 pension and $1,700 Social Security benefit, and Sharon's $900 monthly Social Security benefit. Randy's health has declined severely and he needs to be in the nursing home on Medicaid for long-term care assistance. Because Sharon's own income is less than the MMMNA, she will be able to retain $1,130 of Randy's monthly income; almost all of Randy's remaining income will be directed to paying for his LTC need as his patient's responsibility. (Sharon's income of $900/m plus the $1,130/m equals the MMMNA of $2,030/m)

RAISING THE SPOUSAL DIVERSION ABOVE THE MINIMUM ALLOWANCE

In addition to the Minimum Monthly Maintenance Income Allowance of $2,030/m (until 06/30/18), the income diversion to the community spouse can be increased to the Maximum Monthly Maintenance Income Allowance of $3,022.50/month (until 06/03/18). Medicaid rules allow the income to be increased to the maximum level only through calculating the community spouse's excess shelter costs. Basically, if the community spouse rents their home, has a mortgage, or the housing costs are above a certain level, the spouse can keep more of the institutionalized spouse's income. The rules are generally as follows:

- Housing costs must exceed the community spouse housing allowance of $609/month (2018).
- Housing costs include mortgage payments, rent, insurance, condo maintenance fees and utilities.
- Once the community spouse's shelter costs exceed the allowance of $609/month, the community spouse can start to divert more of the institutionalized spouse's income, up to the maximum level of $3,022.50/month.

CALCULATING THE COMMUNITY SPOUSE'S EXCESS SHELTER COSTS

This will be demonstrated further below and with the worksheet, but this language is extracted from Florida's Medicaid manual:

Step 1: Add the community spouse's monthly housing expenses. Allowed expenses are limited to rent or mortgage payment (including principal and interest), taxes, insurance (homeowners or renters), maintenance charges if a condominium and mandatory homeowner's association fees.

Step 2: To the total obtained above, add the current food stamp standard utility disregard ($347/m for 2018). Allowed utilities are limited to water, sewage, gas, and electric. This basically gives a credit of $347/m for utilities, but if utilities are higher than this, you can raise above the $347.

Step 3: To determine what portion of the total shelter costs is excess, subtract $609 from the total costs. The difference is the community spouse's excess shelter costs.

BEST EXAMPLE OF CALCULATING THE SPOUSAL DIVERSION

This can all be pretty confusing, even to elder law attorneys, so hopefully the following helps. Here, Dad is in the nursing home (the institutionalized spouse) and mom is doing well at home (as the community spouse). They own a home with a mortgage of $800/month. Dad's income is $2,000/month and Mom's income is $1,000/month. Total assets are below $123,600 or they hired an elder law attorney (like us!) to help protect assets over this level.

Without any excess shelter costs, Mom will be able to keep $1,030/month of the husband's income as the Minimum Monthly Maintenance Income Allowance (MMMNA). Dad will keep $105/month as the personal needs allowance and the rest goes to the nursing home as part of the patient's responsibility.

To try to get Mom more income diverted from Dad's own income, we can calculate the excess shelter costs:

    $ 800/m (mortgage)
+$ 150/m (property tax)
+$ 100/m (insurance)
+$ 347/m (Standard Utility Allowance)
=$1,397/m (Total)
- $ 609/m (normal standard housing costs)
=$ 788/m (excess housing costs for the community spouse)

This means we raise the $2,030/month minimum by $788/month. Mom will now keep $2,818/month as she had housing costs exceeding the normal $609/month. The husband keeps $105/month and the nursing home is paid only $77/month! ($3,000 total gross income minus the $2,818 minus the $105 = $77)

ASSETS AND MEDICAID

As Medicaid is a "needs-based" program, most individuals applying for benefits can only have $2,000 in countable assets. The community spouse is allowed to have around $123,600 in countable assets (2018). If both spouses are institutionalized, only $3,000 in countable assets is allowed between them.

Assets may either be countable or non-countable for Medicaid purposes. The most important asset, the homestead, is **not** countable unless it exceeds $572,000 (2018) in value. There are a few other non-countable assets such as:

- Any one car of unlimited value;
- A second car if over seven years old and not a collectible car;
- Funeral plots;
- Irrevocable pre-paid burial policies; and
- Life insurance with face value less than $2,500.

A jointly held bank account is a countable asset and is *not* divided among the owners. Regardless of whether a son or daughter was added to the account and has been funding it to pay the parent's bills, the value of the account is *all* attributed to the applicant unless it can be proven otherwise.

There are many other rules, pages worth, and an amazing number of places where it is possible, or even likely, to make a disqualifying mistake. Legal advice is highly recommended if your assets exceed the bare minimum and you intend to apply for Medicaid.

PATIENT'S RESPONSIBILITY

As discussed, a single Medicaid recipient receives, the recipient may retain $105/month as a "personal needs allowance." The total of the balance must be paid to the nursing home. This portion is known as the "Patient's Responsibility." The allowance the recipient retains is intended to cover haircuts, laundry, and other services and personal items the individual will need each month. This is an absurdly low amount that others (family and friends) will typically supplement. As noted above, a married

Medicaid recipient may be able to divert some or all of their income to their spouse at home.

BASIC MEDICAID APPLICATION PROCEDURE

When an applicant's assets exceed the minimum level discussed above, it is best to hire an elder law attorney to prepare the Medicaid application. The application process can be long, arduous, and confusing. All assets need to be accounted for, accurately valued, and correctly categorized. The requirements are strict, and the timing stringent. Filing an inaccurate application can slow down or even prevent receipt of benefits.

An applicant may receive benefits for the period of up to three months prior to the date of the Medicaid application *if* he or she would have been eligible during that period. If an individual becomes ineligible in a given month, Medicare coverage generally stops at the end of that month.

ASSET PROTECTION STRATEGIES

A number of strategies can protect assets and still enable an individual to be eligible for Medicaid. Each and every case needs individual attention to develop a comprehensive program that best meets the client's needs. Some of the options include the use of Medicaid qualified annuities, strategic gifting, and personal service contracts. These can be set up far in advance of need or even *when the elder is in the nursing home*. Regardless of *when* you choose to set up your asset protection program, a board certified elder law attorney will be with you for every step of the strategic planning, asset coordination, and application processes.

CAN'T I JUST GIVE MY MONEY TO MY CHILDREN IF I GET SICK?

No. You are not allowed to transfer any assets within **five years** of a Medicaid application. Not disclosing such a transfer is a felony.

GIFTING AND ASSET TRANSFERS

Transfer penalties are the greatest limiting factor to efficient asset protection planning. No gifting can be done within five (5) years of an application for Medicaid, although there are exceptions to this rule. More on gifting is in Chapter 16, where you can learn about giving assets to irrevocable trusts five years before you get sick.

MEDICAID PAYS FOR ASSISTED LIVING FACILITIES AND IN-HOME CARE.

Government assistance can also be used when an individual is in an assisted living facility (ALF) or at home, although accessing programs for those "aging-at-home" is even more difficult than nursing home Medicaid. The financial information described above applies to these programs as well. Importantly, these alternative Medicaid programs are not absolute entitlements, meaning wait lists for acceptance on these programs is highly likely. This means that even if all of your funds have been spent, Medicaid may not help you in the assisted living facility or at home.

TRUE STORY

I had a daughter come in to meet regarding her mother who was in the nursing home. The daughter was under serious stress as the Florida Department of Children and Families (DCF) was called on her for possible elder exploitation. When the daughter was visiting her mother in the rehabilitation facility, a social worker pulled the daughter aside and said "I did not tell you this but you need to go to the bank and withdraw all of your mother's money, otherwise the nursing home will take it all." After the daughter went to do this at the bank, the bank called DCF to report possible elder law abuse. As we know, you cannot give all of your assets away in order to get onto Medicaid, but the nursing home social worker, who should know better, almost got my client's daughter arrested!

APPROPRIATE MEDICAID SPEND-DOWN PLANNING

Appropriate spend-down planning generally means legally spending money before Medicaid is applied for. An example of spend-down planning is as follows:

> Sally, age 82, had a stroke and needs long-term care in the nursing home. Sally has a home worth less than $572,000, a car with an outstanding loan of $5,000, and only $10,000 in the bank (i.e., only $10,000 in countable assets). Here, the family can legally spend-down Sally's assets by paying off her car loan of $5,000 and purchasing a pre-paid, irrevocable funeral policy worth $3,000. Sally's bank account will now

have only $2,000 and she will now be eligible for long-term care Medicaid.

This is a simple example of spend-down planning but it shows the legal spending of a small amount of assets that could have been helpful to Sally and her family.

WHEN YOU NEED AN ELDER LAW ATTORNEY FOR MEDICAID

We can generally say that an elder law attorney is necessary to the Medicaid application process when:

- The applicant's countable assets exceed the bare minimum, such as the example above with Sally, to legally protect assets and then apply for Medicaid
- Income exceeds the applicable income cap and a qualified income trust is needed
- The family is confused and needs help in a difficult time. There is no such thing as an easy Medicaid application and getting help from a good elder law attorney can be helpful in all situations
- The spouse at home (the "community spouse") wants or needs to keep more income than Florida allows
- The family has care issues and concerns and does not know where to turn

THE FLORIDA MEDICAID LIEN

After giving my speech on Medicaid at a Caregiver's Conference not far from our office, I was approached by a fellow who asked about Medicaid payback in Florida. His basic statement to me was that "Most people do not know that Medicaid [for the elder] is only a loan to pay for long-term care, not a gift." His basic point was that if the elder is on Medicaid, any leftover assets the decedent owned upon death is subject to a lien by the state of Florida. This is commonly known as the Medicaid "pay-back" or reimbursement provisions, and many people are unaware of this provision in the law.

My answer to him was that he was correct - Florida Medicaid does have a pay-back provision, just like all states. During your lifetime, if you receive Medicaid benefits, if you die after age 55, the State of Florida is a creditor in your estate. The state has a claim in the amount of funds expended for your benefit during your lifetime, who can definitely become a great deal of money if you spend time in long-term care. I told him this was generally not much of an issue in most situations.

First, if the Medicaid applicant was single, he or she was only allowed to have less than $2,000 in countable assets in order to be on Medicaid. This means that the applicant likely has nothing for Medicaid to make a claim against upon the applicant's death. A single applicant is already impoverished and has generally nothing for the state of Florida to take.

Next, even if the decedent owned a homestead property, this property is not subject to creditor's claims (including the state of Florida!) in most circumstances. There are exceptions to this rule though, such as:

- The decedent's property lost its homestead status before death (maybe by renting the home, for instance)

- Not all homestead properties are equal. If the property is a co-operative share, such as in a mobile home park, this does not get statutory protection for Florida homestead purposes.

- The decedent's last will and testament called for the sale of the decedent's home.

Ok, so the Medicaid lien is not an issue in most circumstances. So where would a Medicaid lien take place? We can think about a few circumstances there the lien could/would be applicable:

- The decedent sold their home and went off of Medicaid before death (i.e., the applicant went on private pay)
- The decedent received an inheritance - either before they died or after, which could then be subject to the lien
- The decedent did not disclose or discover all known assets as part of the application process and the assets had to be probated upon death
- The decedent's spouse died first and left money to the Medicaid applicant, who then dies

One big point to be made is that good estate planning can avoid any potential Medicaid lien, regardless. That is one reason to see a good elder law attorney and to make sure the family creates a good estate plan, with a great durable power of attorney, to help avoid any probate or creditor problems upon the elder's death.

In summation, the Medicaid lien is not a worry for most Medicaid applicants if you have a good elder law attorney. This also means that good asset protection planning can protect assets during your lifetime and upon your death.

Key Points to Remember:

- Medicaid planning should be considered in almost all estate plans. Exceptions to this may mean you have sufficient wealth to pay for your long-term care or you do not have heirs you wish to leave money to.

- Protecting assets can be done even when someone is in the nursing home.

- Do not look to friends, family, relatives or even people in the nursing home to provide you advice on Medicaid planning; go see a Board Certified elder law attorney to assist you.

CHAPTER 12
VETERANS BENEFITS AND LONG-TERM CARE

As mentioned previously, long-term care can be very expensive. Medicaid can assist those in need by paying for nursing home, assisted living, and in-home care, although benefits tend to be more limited for assisted living and in-home care. There are, however, other programs which provide for U.S. veterans and their surviving spouses. These are of two types: those which are not dependent on income and those which are.

SERVICE-CONNECTED DISABILITY COMPENSATION:

A Non-Income Dependent Benefit

VA Disability Compensation is a monthly tax-exempt payment to service-disabled veterans, with the payment amount dependent on the disability rating, *not on the basis of need*. A "service-connected disability" is a disability which results from active military service. Disabilities are rated in 10 percent increments, with 0% being "no disability" to 100%, which is totally disabled. The rating describes how severely the disability impacts the veteran's daily life.

Disability compensation payments do not automatically start when a veteran becomes disabled. Application for these benefits is important because documentation of the veteran's disability affects the veteran's cost of VA health services; eligibility for diverse training, healthcare, employment, home loan, and insurance programs; and prioritization for various services.

The application will be reviewed and evaluated. If the VA compensates a veteran for a service-related disability, the veteran may also apply for a Special Monthly Compensation to provide additional monthly monetary payments to pay for needed services if the veteran's disability causes the veteran:

1. To need another person to provide significant help with personal care, or
2. To remain bedridden

Programs Based on Partially on Need

Disability payments are not "needs based," nor is the amount dependent on a veteran's income or assets.

HOME AND COMMUNITY BASED SERVICES

All veterans enrolled for the VA Medical Benefits Package are eligible for Home and Community Based Services, *if* the veteran has a clinical need for the service, it is available in the veteran's location, and the veteran's level of disability justifies the service. The Standard VA Benefit Package includes:

- Geriatric Evaluation to assess care needs and design a care plan
- Adult Day Health Care
- Respite Care
- Skilled Home Health Care

The VA covers nursing home room and board if the veteran meets service connected status, level of disability, and income eligibility criteria. If the veteran lives in an Assisted Living or Adult Family Home, room and board are not covered, but some Home and Community Based Services *will* be covered.

Programs Based on Need

One of the most looked to "needs based" VA programs is the Pension program, which is most often used to help pay to keep someone home or to pay for assisted living for veterans and their spouses.

PENSION

The VA Pension Benefit Program provides a monthly, tax-free, "needs based," monetary payment for:

1. Low-income veterans with wartime service. (Veteran's Pension)
2. The low-income, un-remarried surviving spouse and/or unmarried child(ren) of a deceased veteran with wartime service. (Survivor's Pension)

Who:

- Are age 65 or older, or
- Show evidence of a permanent and total non-service-connected disability, or
- Reside as a patient in a nursing home, or
- Receive Social Security disability benefits.

Generally, the claimant would need assistance with his or her activities of daily living (ADLs), such as bathing, feeding, dressing, or attending to the wants of nature.

Other requirements are that the veteran must meet wartime service requirements, be financially eligible and able to meet an asset (net worth) and income test (below the maximum annual pension rate), and have been discharged for a cause *other than dishonorable*.

Wartime service is defined as having served at least ninety days of active military, naval or air service duty with at least one day served during a time of armed conflict in the following:

- World War II   Dec. 7, 1941 – Dec. 31, 1946
- Korean conflict   June 27, 1950 – Jan. 31, 1955
- Vietnam era   Feb. 28, 1961 – May 7, 1975

  (for Veterans who served in the Republic of Vietnam during that period)

- Otherwise: August 5, 1964 – May 7, 1975
- Gulf War   August 2, 1990 – Feb. 28, 1991

Veterans who began active duty after September 7, 1980, are required to have at least 24 months of active duty service, or, if less than that, to have completed his/her entire tour of active duty.

ASSET AND INCOME LIMITATIONS FOR VA PENSION BENEFITS

Pension was designed to afford beneficiaries a minimum level of security, and not intended to protect substantial assets or build up the beneficiary's estate for the benefit of heirs. In October 2018, the VA imposed a cap of $123,600 in countable assets in order to receive benefits. The VA had never imposed a hard cap on assets and until then, asset limitations were roughly based upon the veteran's age. The asset cap of $123,600, which will increase slightly over the years, does not include the applicant's homestead property. Here, the VA allows a homestead property of any value as long as the lot size is less than two acres.

Countable income is comprised of income from most sources and from any eligible dependents and includes earnings, disability and retirement payments, annuity interest and dividend payments, and net farming or a business income. Unreimbursed medical expenses, in particular, reduce countable income and allow eligibility for Pension. This means that as long as the applicant has high out of pocket medical expenses, there is no practical income limit. The amount of income the VA will pay a Pension applicant is set forth further below.

OTHER PROGRAMS

The VA Pension program contains two additional benefits for elderly veterans/surviving spouses eligible for or receiving a VA Pension Benefit. These benefits [1) Aid and Attendance, and 2) Housebound] increase the amount of Pension paid in order to cover extraordinary healthcare costs.

Aid and Attendance and Housebound allowances increase the size of Pension awarded. Veterans/surviving spouses who are ineligible for a basic pension for the sole reason that their income is too high may be eligible for pension at these higher rates. Eligible claimants cannot receive Aid and Attendance benefits and Housebound benefits at the same time.

AID AND ATTENDANCE (PENSION)

For veterans eligible for or receiving a VA Pension benefit, an additional monetary award, "aid and attendance" may be made to help cover extraordinary health care costs when the claimant (the veteran or his or her surviving spouse) has an incapacity, physical or mental, which requires "care or assistance on a regular basis." Aid and Attendance is awarded according to:

- A claimant's needs and unreimbursed medical expenses, and
- Without considering a claimant's income, as long as medical expenses are high enough, if the claimant:
  √ Requires help performing daily self-care activities, which may include bathing, eating, dressing, toileting, adjusting prosthetic devices; or
  √ Requires protection from the hazards or dangers of his or her daily environment; or
  √ Is bedridden; or
  √ Is a nursing home patient; or
  √ Has corrected visual acuity of 5/200 or less in both eyes; or a concentric visual field contracted to 5 degrees or less.

Aid and Attendance generally can provide cash assistance *up to* the following amounts (2018):

Single Veteran	$1,829/month
Married Veteran	$2,169/month
Surviving Spouse	$1,176/month

Aid and Attendance is probably the best program available to help the family pay for assisted living, nursing home, and expensive in-home care.

HOUSEBOUND

Housebound increases the monthly pension amount for a veteran/ surviving spouse substantially confined to his or her home due to permanent disability. Evidence of eligibility for increased housebound disability pension benefits must demonstrate that the claimant has:

- A single permanent 100 percent disabling disability AND that disability causes the claimant to be permanently and substantially confined to his or her immediate premises; or
- A significant (rated 60% or higher) additional disability over and above the disability used to establish pension eligibility

HOW IS PENSION CALCULATED?

Your monthly Pension amount will then be calculated as the amount equal to the difference between your countable family income and the annual Pension benefits mentioned above. For these purposes, if a veteran or his or her surviving spouse needs help with their activities of daily living, has assets below the asset threshold ($123,600 in 2018) and has not made any transfers/gifts in the last three years, the VA will provide a cash Pension under the following example:

> Dad, a veteran, is living in an assisted living facility that costs $4,500 per month. Dad's income is $2,000 per month from his social security. Dad needs help

with two of his activities of daily living and has assets below $123,600. Here, the VA will provide a Pension payment in the amount of $1,829 per month, which will substantially help pay for his assisted living facility.

NEW VA GIFTING PENALTY

The VA made substantial changes to their Pension rules in October, 2018. Here, they applied the asset limit of $123,600. They also put in a transfer penalty for giving assets away. The VA never had a formal transfer penalty before this time, unlike Medicaid and their five-year lookback period. The VA's new transfer penalty basically applies a penalty for giving assets away (i.e., transfers) within three years of an application for VA benefits. If a gift was done, the VA will assess a transfer penalty of dividing the gifted amount by the maximum annual Pension rate ($2,169/m in 2018). An example of this is as follows:

> Dad has $150,000 in countable assets. He gives away $30,000 to his son and applies for VA benefits six months later. Due to this gift, the VA will apply a gift penalty of some 13.8 months, meaning the veteran will not be eligible for Pension benefits for 13.8 months from the date of the application. (30,000 divided by 2,169 = 13.8)

If your elder is looking to get VA Pension benefits, hiring an elder law attorney may help you or your loved one:

1. Legally spend any "excess" funds impeding your eligibility,
2. Set up an irrevocable trust three years before VA benefits are wanted, and
3. Identify specific VA programs for which you may be eligible.

Key Points to Remember:

- Don't forget about VA benefits as part of your long-term care planning.

- VA Pension benefits, especially Aid and Attendance, is a great way to pay for long-term care, which can include independent living and the assisted living facility.

- Pension, especially Aid and Attendance, can be most useful for assisted living benefits from the VA.

- While not always necessary, an elder law attorney can help spot which particular VA benefits you may be eligible for.

CHAPTER 13
COMMON QUESTIONS AND ANSWERS ON MEDICAID AND VA BENEFITS

WHEN IT COMES to accessing government benefits to pay for long-term care, there is a great deal of misleading and confusion information out there. While every situation is different, the following is a list of common questions and answers we receive on a daily basis.

WHAT HAPPENS TO MY HOME IF I GO ONTO MEDICAID?

The rules for Medicaid and homestead in Florida have different rules depending on if you are single or married.

If you are married, the spouse can live there and there are no potential problems or hitches for the homestead property. There is not asset limit here and the cost of the home may help the community spouse keep more income. We may be concerned if the spouse at home - the community spouse - were to predecease the Medicaid recipient, but that is another issue.

If the Medicaid applicant is single and needs Medicaid in the nursing home or assisted living facility, the applicant is allowed to own a home of up to $572,000 in value (2018). Even if the applicant never returns to the home, the homestead is protected and will never be made a countable asset for Medicaid purposes (unless rented!). Upon the applicant's death, the homestead is protected from creditors, including the state of Florida, if it descends to your heirs at law. Problems occur though because all of your income goes to the nursing home as part of your patient's responsibility. This means that the family will have to pay for the home's mortgage, upkeep, insurance, taxes, etc., as your assets have been depleted and your income goes to the nursing home! Renting the home is possible but this removes the homestead protection, so that can be an issue as well.

THE INCOME RULES FOR MEDICAID ARE CONFUSING - GO THROUGH THEM AGAIN?

Income rules for long-term care Medicaid have a number of moving parts that vary based upon marital status.

A single person on Medicaid in the nursing home must pay their countable income to the facility as part of his "patient's responsibility." In effect, the Medicaid applicant must pay their income to the facility as part of their co-pay, where Medicaid pays the rest of the funds for the resident's stay. The single applicant is allowed to keep $105/month as part of his "personal needs allowance." This allows the resident to buy personal items such as clothing and toiletries.

A married person in the nursing home has the same set of rules with one large qualification - the spouse at home may be able to keep some of the applicant's income as part of the community spouse's income allowance (CSIA). The community spouse may be able to siphon off some of the applicant's income based upon the community spouse's own income. An example of this is as follows:

Married nursing home resident with $2,000/month income applies for Medicaid. The spouse at home (the community spouse) only has income of $1,000/month. The spouse at home, as a minimum, may keep $1,030/month of the resident's income, at a minimum. This amount varies annually (see below for up-to-date numbers). This means that the nursing home resident can keep $105 per month as their personal needs allowance, paying $865/m to the nursing home as their patient's responsibility. ($2,000 minus $1030 minus $105 = $865).

If the applicant's gross income exceeds $2250/month, they will need a Qualifed Income Trust(QIT). The QIT generally does not affect where the income goes (i.e., to the nursing home/community spouse) but how it gets there.

HOW ARE IRAS COUNTED FOR MEDICAID PURPOSES?

When an elderly or disabled person is looking to apply for long-term care Medicaid in Florida, the applicant must document their income and assets for Medicaid purposes, which are set forth in our asset and income levels webpage.

Part of the application process means looking at countable assets. Countable assets include bank accounts, stocks, bonds, mutual funds, annuities and more. Basically, the applicant must disclose all assets as part of the process. Interestingly and importantly, the applicant's IRA/401K/Qualified Plans may not be a countable asset for application purposes. The rule is that if the applicant is taking periodic distributions from their IRA/401K/Qualified Plans, the account is not a countable asset for Medicaid purposes. Instead, any distributions from the account are counted as income for Medicaid. This would mean, for instance, that any distribution from the IRA/401K/Qualified Plan may go to the nursing home as part of the patient's responsibility. This would also mean that any distributions from these plans could require a Qualified Income Trust, among other important ramifications. An example for Medicaid purposes is as follows:

> Example #1: Mom is an unmarried nursing home resident and has $50,000 in her checking account and $50,000 in stocks and bonds. Her gross income is $2,000/month from Social Security. In order to get mom onto Medicaid, she is only allowed $2,000 in countable assets, meaning that she must spend down most of her assets (some $98,000) before Medicaid will assist her.

> Example #2: Same facts but mom only has $10,000 in her checking account and $90,000 in her IRA. If mom is taking period distributions of $300/month from her IRA, she will only have the checking account as a countable asset for Medicaid purposes, with the IRA not counting as an asset. Interestingly, the $300/month coming from the IRA will take mom over the income cap for Medicaid purposes. Also, any distributions from the IRA will be countable income for Medicaid purposes.

In both examples, your elder would want to see a good elder law attorney to assist with the Medicaid application. In example #1, the elder law attorney may be able to help the elder legally spend down the assets. In example #2, an elder law attorney would be needed to help establish the Qualified Income Trust.

CAN I GIVE AWAY $15,000 PER YEAR TO PROTECT IT FROM THE NURSING HOME?

No! We get this question all of the time. Many people are concerned about protecting their assets in the event they go into the nursing home. We all know that the nursing home is very expensive, often exceeding $9,000 per month. Of course, none of us ever want to go into the nursing home, but sometimes this is the only place that can provide the correct care for an aging loved one. But the $15,000 per year annual exclusion (2018) relates only to the Federal estate tax annual limit, not to the rules of Medicaid.

Basically, the $15,000 annual gift tax exclusion has nothing to do with the Medicaid 5 year lookback. The Florida rule is that you are not allowed to give away any money if you apply for Medicaid within 5 years of the last gift. This makes sense as the government wants to discourage asset protection or people intentionally impoverishing themselves. If you give money away, the gifting creates a transfer penalty, discussed earlier in this book.

If you want to protect your assets from the nursing home, there are some good ways to do it with good advice from a qualified elder law attorney, as as through irrevocable trust planning as set forth in Chapter 16. But gifting the assets away at $15,000 per year is generally not the way to do it. Giving assets away should be done in a lump sum in certain scenarios, and if you want to try to protect money from the nursing home, would generally be done to an irrevocable asset protection trust.

WILL MY LOVED ONE GET GOOD CARE ON MEDICAID?

We know that many people end up on Medicaid in the nursing home due to the high cost of nursing home care, which can exceed $9,000 per month. But will Medicaid affect your loved one's care?

First, it is illegal for a nursing home or other care provider to discriminate against a patient due to pay or source. This means that the nursing home care providers do not care if your loved one is there through Medicaid or through private pay. I once had a nursing home owner tell me that they preferred Medicaid as a payor source over people privately paying as they knew Medicaid would pay them while the private payers would not always be as forthcoming with the funds.

Next, whether a nursing home accepts Medicaid does not dictate whether it is a good or bad facility. There are 83 nursing homes in Pinellas County, for instance, and all 83 nursing homes accept Medicaid.

Also, Medicaid also will not dictate where your loved one will receive care. This means that you can pick any nursing home you want and the state of Florida does not care. Each facility, however, may have a limit as to the number of Medicaid beds, so depending upon the time of year, there may be a wait list for Medicaid beds.

The truth about Medicaid and Medicaid planning in Florida is that protecting assets with an elder law attorney will not affect your loved one's care, although it may affect placement issues at certain times.

One final piece to this puzzle is that getting good care in any nursing home or assisted living facility is not easy. Care will vary based upon the nursing home staff, doctors, CNAs, administration, corporate governance and more. This is why we have a care coordinator on staff as part of our life care planning practice. Our care coordinator's job is to help you and your loved one get good care in the right facility. Our care coordinator has been a social worker in local nursing homes for over 30 years and she knows what good care looks like. With our law firm, you will not need to worry about good care for your loved one, or the stress of being an advocate, all alone in the medical system, without help.

HOW ARE JOINTLY HELD ASSETS COUNTED FOR MEDICAID PURPOSES?

When someone it looking to apply for Medicaid for a loved one, one of the inevitable questions we get usually sounds something like this:

"I am a joint owner on my mother's bank accounts. Are half of the accounts mine for Medicaid purposes?"

The short answer here is that it is only an asset if the other account owner contributed monies to the account(s). The question here is rooted in ownership of the bank account. It is very common for an elder, rightly or wrongly, to add a child as co-owner of their bank accounts in the event they have a decline in health and need someone to pay their bills.

For Medicaid purposes, a joint owner on a bank account is not considered a partial owner for Medicaid purposes. The law presumes that if the Medicaid applicant is on the financial account, they are a 100% owner. Of course, this is usually true as the account is usually the elder's asset and the child was assed for convenience purposes. If, however, the child could show that some or all of the money was the Medicaid applicants, then the asset can be excluded.

SHOULD I GET DIVORCED FROM MY SPOUSE IN ORDER TO PROTECT OUR ASSETS FROM THE NURSING HOME?

I once had a client come in concerned about his wife's mental and physical decline. The wife had advancing dementia and was in the nursing home. The husband was concerned that all of their assets would be used for his wife's care. In this situation, the husband living at home is known as the "community spouse" and he is allowed to own a house, a car, and up to $123,600 in countable assets (2018). In this case, the husband's countable assets were above the limit to allow his wife to qualify for Medicaid.

In discussing options for protecting his assets while getting his wife onto Medicaid, the husband brought up the concept of a "Medicaid Divorce." The husband had researched this on the internet and had some questions on what this is and how it worked.

I had never actually heard or used the term "Medicaid divorce" so I thought he was referring to a planning technique we generally refer to as "spousal refusal." Spousal refusal is a legal way to protect assets for the community spouse in certain situations. We do not take this technique lightly as it means that the husband would sign a statement saying that he refuses to support his wife. When this is done, the state of Florida would count institutionalized spouse (the spouse in the nursing home) as a single person for Medicaid purposes, which means the community spouse (the husband) would not have to "spend down" his assets until reaching the $123,600 mark (2018). We are frequently hesitant to bring this up as an option as there is an unsavory aspect to tell a spouse that they should sign paperwork that they are not going to support their loved ones.

As we discussed the client's information further, the husband had lots of questions on the Medicaid divorce, who would know this happened, and a number of other things. After going through this for a while, I realized the husband thought that an actual divorce would occur with the Florida court system. This could not be furthest from the truth! We would never encourage a married couple to divorce over Medicaid/nursing home expenses. There are plenty of planning techniques to help the community spouse get their loved ones onto Medicaid, but these options do not include any kind of divorce! The moral of the story is do not believe everything you read on the internet! The husband was very sad that he would either have to divorce his wife or lose all of their assets to the nursing home, and I got to explain that this was not the case at all, much to his relief!

With the Medicaid planning technique known as spousal refusal, the community spouse would typically sign a statement that he or she refuses to support the sick spouse. When this is done, the sick spouse is treated as a single person for Medicaid purposes, meaning the assets of the community spouse are not counted as assets for Medicaid purposes. The state of Florida is also assigned the right to sue the community spouse for refusing to support his or her spouse. Using spousal refusal would likely take place, for instance, in the event of a second marriage situation.

DOES MEDICAID PAY FOR IN-HOME LONG-TERM CARE?

Yes, but the benefits are limited and there is a fairly long wait-list. The income and asset rules are the same for accessing other long-term care Medicaid, but state funding provides for long wait-lists that take only the sickest people. We rarely see people get Medicaid long-term care at home for a variety of reasons.

DO I NEED AN ATTORNEY TO APPLY FOR VA BENEFITS?

The short answer is "maybe."

VA Pension benefits were created to assist with the veteran, and his or her surviving spouse's, extraordinary health care needs. Most people refer to this program as "aid and attendance", which is a specific benefit level for those needing the most help. We have more about veteran's benefits for the elderly here.

VA Pension benefits are "needs based", meaning the applicant must have only a certain amount of countable assets. The VA rules basically want the applicant to need the money for their healthcare but that the funds are not intended to provide an inheritance to the children. This means that the applicant is allowed countable asset limits based upon the applicant's age and money they are spending on their healthcare. For instance, a 65 year old veteran may be allowed $80,000 in countable assets but a 90 year old veteran applying for pension may only be allowed to have $30,000 in assets.

So the general rule is that an elder law attorney is not needed to apply for VA benefits if the assets are already within the applicable range. Here, we typically send people to their local

COMMON QUESTIONS AND ANSWERS ON MEDICAID AND VA BENEFITS

Veterans Services office provided by the county. If the applicant has assets over the limit, then an elder law attorney can help protect assets and only then apply for VA benefits. A good elder law attorney can protect assets with:

- legal gifting;
- asset restructuring;
- irrevocable trust planning;
- and more.

One key to all this planning is that whatever is done to protect assets must not interfere with potential Medicaid benefits in the future. We typically use VA Pension benefits to help with in-home and assisted living care while we generally look to Medicaid to pay for the nursing home.

What does this all mean? If your elder is a veteran or is the surviving spouse of a war-time veteran, you should see an accredited Veteran's Benefits attorney to help clarify your situation and if an attorney is needed.

SECTION 4

PRE-PLANNING FOR LONG-TERM CARE

Chapter 14
Incapacity Planning:
Durable Powers of Attorney and Advance Directives

Chapter 15
Who to Name in Your Incapacity Documents

Chapter 16
Irrevocable Trust Planning Five Years Before You Need Medicaid

CHAPTER 14

INCAPACITY PLANNING: DURABLE POWERS OF ATTORNEY AND ADVANCE DIRECTIVES

> I helped a really nice fellow create a power of attorney for his sick wife. His wife had advancing dementia and was in a nursing home. We were lucky that she had the capacity to name him as her power of attorney due to her declining mental status.
>
> The husband had his own health issues, suffering from emphysema and other ailments while trying to care for his wife and run his business. I impressed upon him the need to create his own incapacity documents due to his failing health, but he put it off.
>
> Of course, we received a call from his niece a few months later. Our client was in the hospital and needed a power of attorney. The niece, who lived out of town, wanted to make sure someone could oversee her uncle's care and provide guidance for the employees of his business.
>
> By the time we went and saw our client, he was not mentally competent to make a power of attorney. His lack of incapacity planning and procrastination in preparing for the future left a mess for our client, his niece, and his incapacitated spouse that could have easily been avoided with good planning.

INCAPACITY PLANNING: DURABLE POWERS OF ATTORNEY AND ADVANCE DIRECTIVES

Good estate planning requires preparation for both your incapacity as well as for your death. (If talking about death wasn't already hard enough, talking about being incapacitated is almost more frightening.) Except in the case of sudden, unexpected death, there is a high potential for a period of incapacitation of indeterminate length before the individual actually dies. There is a 50/50 chance that you will develop some form of dementia before you die so this planning can greatly aid you and your family during your lifetime.

Incapacity means that the individual is partially or fully not able to care for him/herself. In Florida, if an individual is legally incapacitated (partially or totally), the court may appoint a guardian (friend, relative, or professional) to make decisions for the incapacitated person. The guardian appointment process can be lengthy, expensive, and onerous, and *especially* frustrating since the incapacitated individual needs help *immediately*, and the appointment process is not responsive to the urgency of the situation.

If the individual (before incapacitation) has set a healthcare surrogate and a durable power of attorney, guardianship will likely not be needed. Though no one plans to become incapacitated, good incapacity planning can eliminate or minimize a lot of difficulty and/or financial burden for you and your family.

Three documents are highly recommended to structure and establish a comprehensive and efficient incapacity planning program: the durable power of attorney, the health care surrogate and the living will. Failure to set up these end-of-life care documents before they are needed can result in legal bills that easily run into the thousands of dollars, potentially causing you and your family untold problems, expenses and heartache.

DURABLE POWER OF ATTORNEY

FOR MOST PEOPLE, the durable power of attorney, sometimes called a financial power of attorney, is the most important estate-planning instrument available—even more useful than a Last Will and Testament. A durable power of attorney appoints the person of your choice—your "attorney-in-fact"—to act in your place if and when you ever become incapacitated. Powers of attorney are effective immediately upon execution of the document. A "durable" power of attorney means that the power survives your incapacity; e.g., a stroke or dementia.

Your power of attorney can give your attorney-in-fact the ability to pay your bills, manage your assets, deal with insurance issues, protect your assets in the event you are in a nursing home, avoid Medicaid spend-down requirements and much more.

Your power of attorney should be updated periodically for two reasons. One is that powers of attorney change over time. Our standard power of attorney form we use today is better than the power of attorney we were using even five (5) years ago. Each year that goes by brings more opportunities to strengthen our power of attorney document. The other reason is a concern is that your power of attorney also goes "stale" over time. After a number of years, financial institutions may refuse to accept older documents. While this is not legally correct, we recommend updating your durable power of attorney every ten (10) years or sooner, especially when there is a health emergency.

Your attorney-in-fact must be completely trustworthy and faithful to you. If you have any doubts as to whether or not this person will uphold these obligations in your best interest, then we can suggest alternate agents, based upon your situation.

INCAPACITY PLANNING: DURABLE POWERS OF ATTORNEY AND ADVANCE DIRECTIVES

Also, a well-written power of attorney document names alternate agents who can act in the event your first choice is unable to assume responsibilities, and you, being incapacitated, are not able to select a backup yourself. We have seen many powers-of-attorney which fail to appoint alternate agents—if the single designated agent should be unable to act on your behalf and you have not identified an alternate agent, the court will appoint a guardian . . . and you are back where you didn't want to be.

The reality is that not all attorneys are equal and not all powers of attorney are equal. The best powers of attorney require up-to-date legal knowledge, in-depth experience, and a passion to deliver strong, seamless support for you and your family. A well-crafted, comprehensive document can protect you through decades, if need be.

Beyond the durable power of attorney, a complete estate plan should also include both a designation of health care surrogate and a living will. These documents are generally referred to as *advanced directives* and work together in the event you become incapacitated.

PRO TIP ON POWERS OF ATTORNEY

Do not rely upon powers of attorney that come from the internet, your financial institution, Office Depot or even from an attorney who does not specialize in estate planning or elder law. I see bad and ineffectual powers of attorney all of the time, often to devastating consequences for the entire family. Go see an elder law attorney to get the best power of attorney for you and your situation.

DESIGNATION OF A HEALTH CARE SURROGATE

A Designation of Health Care Surrogate names an individual who can help make your medical decisions and communicate with doctors. The document gives your agent the authority to make health care decisions and end-of-life decisions. We frequently refer to your healthcare surrogate as your "promise keeper" who will make sure your wishes are followed at the appropriate time.

In thinking about who to appoint as your healthcare surrogate, please ask yourself the following questions. Remember, this is the person who will speak for you if you are not able to speak for yourself:

- o Have you asked if the individual would be willing to speak on your behalf?
- o Would the individual be able to act on your wishes and separate his/her own feelings from yours?
- o Does the individual live close by or will he or she be able to travel to be at your side if needed?
- o Does the individual know you well and understand what is important to you?
- o Can you trust them trust with your life?
- o Will the individual talk with you now about sensitive issues and listen to your wishes?
- o Will the individual likely be available long into the future?
- o Will the individual be able to handle conflicting opinions between family members, friends, and medical staff?

o Can the individual be a strong advocate for you in the face of unresponsive doctors or institutional personnel?

Most people choose the individual(s) they know best—a spouse or close relative(s) or friend(s)—but, there is no one correct choice.

The Designation of Health Care Surrogate has had a recent change in Florida law that can be helpful to almost everyone. This change went in to effect October, 2015. Under the old rules, the Designation of Health Care Surrogate only went into effect when you became incapacitated. This would seem to make sense as you should be in charge of your own health care decisions while you are able. One problem with this was that your surrogate would not be able to talk to your health care providers due to the HIPAA privacy laws until you were declared incompetent. The other problem was that it is not always easy to decide when someone was incompetent. People have both good and bad days when they have dementia so declaring someone incapable of making healthcare decisions can be difficult.

The changes to the law Designation of Health Care Surrogate allow the surrogate to talk with the principal's health care providers without having to have the principal being declared incompetent. Further, the surrogate can now make the principal's healthcare decisions even without the principal being declared incompetent. This can be very helpful to the entire family as better access to healthcare in emergency situations and other situations. We highly recommend new health care surrogates for our clients.

LIVING WILL

The other piece of your Advanced Directives "package" is your *Living Will*. This legal document provides direction regarding the medical treatment if you are incapacitated at the end of your life. In the event you are not able to make your own healthcare decisions due to your incapacity, your healthcare surrogate is bound to follow your end-of-life wishes as set forth in your living will. This contains the "pull the plug" type desires, and instructions regarding withholding or administering water and food.

A living will allows you to document your wishes concerning medical treatment at the end of life. Living wills are a very important piece to your estate plan, but it should be noted that a living will does not replace the conversation you should have with your healthcare surrogate and your family. A living will cannot take into account all of your desires, wishes, and it will not be able to succinctly say what gives you a quality of life. This is what your conversation with your family will do – give clarification and strength to your living will.

Key Points to Remember:

- A durable power of attorney is, by far, one of the most important documents you can create.
- You should update your power of attorney at least every 10 years.
- Have a qualified attorney create your durable power of attorney.
- Everyone should have a designation of health care surrogate and living will.

> Having a living will is not enough – you need to make sure your family has a copy of your living will and that you have discussed your wishes with your children.

Conclusion

- Do you have a durable power of attorney created by an attorney?
- Is your durable power of attorney less than 10 years old?
- Do you have an updated Designation of Healthcare Surrogate?
- Do you have a Living Will?
- Have you talked with your family about your end of life wishes?

CHAPTER 15

WHO TO NAME IN YOUR INCAPACITY DOCUMENTS

You absolutely must trust your fiduciaries (your successor trustee, personal representative, attorney-in-fact, healthcare surrogate) to act fairly and in your, and your estate's best interests. There is no better way to destroy an estate plan than when untrustworthy family members gain power upon your incapacity or death. Consider other choices, if you have any doubts about a family member's:

- ability to remain impartial
- wisdom and intellectual abilities
- decision making capability
- sense of responsibility
- financial savvy
- trustworthiness
- job/family stability
- or other concerns . . .

Remember, you can choose a professional fiduciary, such as an attorney or accountant, to assist you and your family. While there is a cost to naming a professional fiduciary in your estate plan, you should rest easy knowing that a professional will be there to assist your family and comply with your wishes.

HEALTHCARE SURROGATE SELECTION

In general, you should not name co-powers of attorney or co-healthcare surrogates. In the event you become incapacitated, you should only have one trusted person who will be in charge of your financial and healthcare decisions. Except in limited circumstances, naming multiple contemporaneous (at the same time) agents is an invitation to disagreements and problems, delays in fulfillment of your wishes, and confusion, all of which good planning certainly tries to avoid.

If you have multiple people who would be appropriate to represent you in the event of your incapacity, you may want to consider naming ONE person to fulfill the role, with others as sequential backups. Each alternate would have NO power unless and until the preceding designated individual was unable or unwilling to fulfill power of attorney responsibilities.

Selecting your fiduciaries is both a logical and an emotional decision, but the emotional part may be difficult to determine, because logic is telling you what you *should* do. You may lay out the pros and cons logically based on various individuals intellect and legal/medical knowledge, their personal integrity, their physical proximity/availability, or how emotionally "close" you are, but often it is a good idea to "sleep" on big decisions in order to access your emotional barometer. When you *think* you have made the right decision, concentrate on it before you go to sleep. If you waken in the middle of the night thinking, "no!," you might want to look further.

WHY SLEEP ON IT?

When you are awake, you tend to think logically, and your logical mind will argue that it *knows* the answers. It will also block your emotions. When you sleep, that wall of consciousness comes down, and you are able to access how you *really feel* about something. That middle of the night feeling can often tell you something of which your conscious mind is not aware.

As part of any good estate plan, you should review your choices with your attorney to make sure you have made the best decision possible make and sure that the individuals you would like to serve as your fiduciaries agree to fulfill the roles.

TRUE STORY

I had an elderly client with advanced dementia. She was well provided for in her assisted living facility, communicative, but had no short-term memory.

This woman had two sons: one lived up north, the other moved to the area to care for her and served as my client's power of attorney and health care surrogate. The two sons did not get along and did not even talk to each other. The son up north did not like the fact that that his brother was "in charge" of his incapacitated mother and flew down to visit. He hired an attorney to meet his mother at the assisted living facility, and a "psychiatrist" to determine if his mother was competent. Mom refused to revoke the old power of attorney, but did agree to add the two sons as co-powers of attorney, where they could only act together on all matters.

When I got involved, I let the other attorney know how he had created a giant mess. If the two brothers refused to talk with each other, how could they possibly act together to make their mom's health and financial decisions? It was pure idiocy and plain bad lawyering. Luckily, I was able to resolve matters for my client's benefit.

WHO TO NAME IN YOUR INCAPACITY DOCUMENTS

IF you are having a difficult time selecting individuals for their roles as your fiduciaries, try "backing" into the answer by compiling your list of people first before deciding what you want them to do.

1. Who excels at being impartial?

2. Who do you admire for their wisdom and intellectual abilities?

3. Who is great at making decisions?

4. Who do you know who takes responsibility seriously?

5. Who has great financial savvy?

6. Who is the most trustworthy?

7. Who has job, family, and personal stability?

8. Who can you trust to be loyal to you and your wishes over their own personal perspectives?

CHAPTER 16

IRREVOCABLE TRUST PLANNING FIVE YEARS BEFORE YOU NEED MEDICAID

MEDICAID IN FLORIDA

Let's say you live in a state where the average monthly cost of nursing home care is $8,000. Three years ago, you gifted $400,000 of your estate to your children, making the decision that you would retain $100,000 to cover your living expenses over and above your Social Security benefits. Two years ago, you fell and broke your hip badly enough that the nursing home became your permanent residence. Your $100,000 nest egg gave only 12 months in the nursing home. Now comes the penalty part. Since you gave away $400,000 within five years of going into the nursing home and the average cost of nursing home care is $8,000, you will be ineligible for Medicaid for the number of months of nursing home care that money would have paid for—50 months. The period of ineligibility does not start when you enter the nursing home. It starts after you have:

1) Moved into the nursing home,

2) Reduced your assets to the limit set for Medicaid eligibility,

3) Applied for Medicaid, and

> 4) Received approval.
>
> So who is going to pay for the cost of your nursing home care for the next four plus years? Not Medicaid. And you don't have the money because you gave it away.

Most people who have accumulated a notable amount of assets over their lifetimes want to do *something* to prevent their life savings from being drained away to cover the high cost of long-term care should they need it. But, what to do? One of the first rules to know: If you want to qualify for Medicaid, you are not allowed to give your assets away within five (5) years of applying for nursing home admission. That five years is Medicaid's "lookback" period, and there are penalties for violating it which can seriously affect you and your family.

So the question is what, if anything, can you do to protect your assets? One of the first and most important things you can do is create a great estate plan, including a good durable power of attorney. A good power of attorney is one of the keys to almost all asset protection strategies.

After preparing through good estate planning, you may want to consider giving money away before you need nursing home care. If you do not have children that you want to leave an inheritance, then you should not worry about this. If, however, you want to try and leave money for heirs, giving money away may be the best way to proceed. Ideally, an aging parent would implement a plan to protect his or her assets for his/her children five years before needing long-term care. But life is rarely that easy. How are you to know where you will be five years from now? This is where an Irrevocable Asset Protection Trust may help you and your family.

WHAT IS AN IRREVOCABLE ASSET PROTECTION TRUST?

A trust transfers asset ownership from one individual (the trustmaker/settlor) to an individual (the trustee) who is charged to use the assets for the benefit of another individual or group of people (the beneficiaries). The "trust instrument" or the "trust agreement" is a document that outlines the trustee's responsibilities and the beneficiaries rights.

There are two types of trusts. A "Revocable Living Trust" which allows you to designate how your assets will be distributed upon your death without being required to go through probate. You will own the trust, which leaves the trust assets exposed to creditors, but you will still have the power to change, rescind, or revoke the trust, if desired. A Revocable Living Trust is a probate and estate planning device; it is not an asset protection device. Assets in a Revocable Living Trust are not protected from the cost of long-term care.

An Irrevocable Asset Protection Trust, on the other hand, is an effective way to protect assets from the costs of the nursing home, primarily because, once placed in such a trust, the assets no longer legally belong to the trustmaker.

WHY USE AN IRREVOCABLE ASSET PROTECTION TRUST?

Irrevocable Asset Protection Trusts are generally used as a way to "set aside" assets so they are not counted as assets which must be "spent down" in order to qualify for Medicaid or Veteran's benefits, and so they can be passed on to the asset owner's heirs.

The owner of the assets who places these assets into an Irrevocable Asset Protection Trust will: 1) no longer have control of the assets, except in the sense that the trustmaker may change beneficiaries upon their death, and 2) cannot be a beneficiary of that trust, except for, perhaps, having limited rights to the income from the trust. An unfunded trust provides no protection. The trust can only protect assets after they have been transferred to the trust.

In order for the Irrevocable Asset Protection Trust to protect your assets, you, as settlor, must have;

1. No power to revoke, rescind, or amend the trust, nor retain any right to reclaim trust assets.
2. No power to determine how the trust will be managed or the assets invested.
3. No significant power over the trust. You cannot be the trustee of the trust.
4. Set up and transferred your assets to the trust within five years of an application for nursing home benefits. It cannot be done on the eve of going into the nursing home, for instance.

The key advantages of an Irrevocable Asset Protection Trusts are that:

1. They protect your heirs from the heavy taxation that would result if you gave them substantial gifts outright.

2. The gifted assets are generally held by a single trustee so that your children do not receive and squander all of the assets before your death.
3. Under certain circumstances, if you have a health problem within the next five (5) years, the assets can be returned and protected in alternate ways.
4. Monies held in trust are not at risk should your children divorce, owe creditors, or become incapacitated.
5. You can retain the income stream from the trust during your lifetime and still qualify for Medicaid.

SHOULD I CREATE AN IRREVOCABLE ASSET PROTECTION TRUST?

If you have substantial assets that you want to protect for your children's benefit, an irrevocable asset protection trust can be an invaluable tool. The key constraint is that you must be willing to give up control of a portion of your estate before you get sick. It is also critical that you trust the trustee of the trust.

EXAMPLE OF IRREVOCABLE ASSET PROTECTION TRUST PLANNING

Joe, age 86, is doing well health wise. He has three children and $500,000 in stock and other investments. Joe knows that long-term care would be expensive and he wants to make sure he leaves something to his children. After consultation, Joe decides that he would like to try to protect $400,000 by giving it to a trust he established. He names his son as trustee of that trust during his lifetime. Joe can keep the income produced by the trust but the principal produced is protected. Also, Joe kept some $100,000 in his own name in case he got sick or wanted to spend his own money. After five years from the gift of assets to the trust, these funds will be protected from being spent for the nursing home.

WHEN SHOULD I CREATE AN IRREVOCABLE ASSET PROTECTION TRUST?

Ideally an Irrevocable Asset Protection Trust is created five (5) years before you need long-term care.

Key Points to Remember:

- If you have liquid assets exceeding $200,000 and you want to protect assets for your heirs, an *Irrevocable Asset Protection Trust* may be beneficial.
- You must trust any child you create an asset trust with.
- You should look at doing an *Irrevocable Asset Protection Trust* before you get sick.
- Your *Irrevocable Asset Protection Trust* may also protect your home in the event you needed a long-term stay in the nursing home.

SECTION 5

FINDING HELP

Chapter 17
Choosing the Right Attorney for You

Chapter 18
Finding Local Services

Chapter 19
My Elder Just Went to the Nursing Home:
What Should I do Next?

CHAPTER 17
CHOOSING THE RIGHT ATTORNEY FOR YOU

The reality is that not all attorneys are created equal. Of course, not all attorneys practice estate planning. Many attorneys work in many different areas of the law and attorneys who work in multiple areas, including estate planning, likely will not have the specialized knowledge needed to assist you. Also, not all estate planning attorneys know a great deal about elder law issues and not all elder law attorneys work in the estate planning arena as well. I know this because I see other attorneys' work product and the problems that they can create with improper advice.

When looking to meet with an elder law attorney, you should consider the following questions. Ask yourself, does the attorney have the following attributes?

Important attributes for your elder law attorney:	Yes	No
Are they Board Certified by the Florida Bar Association in Elder Law?		
Are they VA Accredited?		
Do they offer a flat fee schedule for work?		
Do they offer free initial office consultation?		
Do they give free seminars to the public?		
Do they give continuing education to the legal community?		
Do they employ a social worker/care coordinator on staff?		
Do they practice exclusively in estate planning and elder law?		
Does their AVVO web page show good client reviews?		
Have they authored useful books regarding elder law and estate planning?		
Are they friendly and approachable?		
Do they volunteer in the community?		
Does their law firm have an excellent reputation?		

CHAPTER 18

FINDING LOCAL SERVICES

WHEN YOU ARE dealing with an aging loved one, it is very difficult to receive good information. Our opinion is that your elder law attorney should be the starting point. Whether you have a little or a lot of money, a good elder law attorney will be able to review your loved one's incapacity documents, estate plans and will also discuss ways to pay for long-term care. After that, here is some good information on places to start:

ELDERCARE LOCATOR

The Eldercare Locator is a nationwide service that connects older Americans and their caregivers with information on senior services, **including Area Agencies on Aging.** This is a government website.

NH COMPARE

Nursing Home Compare has detailed information about every Medicare and Medicaid-certifiednursing homein the country. This is a government website.

FLORIDA NURSING HOME RATINGS

This website provides a ratings list for nursing home/SNF facilities at http://www.floridahealthfinder.gov/LandingPages/NursingHomeGuide.aspx This is a government website.

GENWORTH COST OF CARE

This website provides information on the cost of long-term care in every state.

ASSISTED LIVING DATA

The directory on this site allows for a search of residential facilities by Zip Code or State and does not require personal information. This is NOT a government website.

FLORIDA SHINE OFFICES

The Florida SHINE program provides trained volunteers to help consumers understand various types of insurance for older persons. This is an excellent place to get unbiased advice based upon your particular circumstances.

MEDICAID OFFICES

Medicaid.Gov has basic information on Medicaid programs in every state and links to state Medicaid websites. This is a government website. The reality is that the State of Florida's Medicaid office **will not be helpful** to you or your loved one.

Conclusion

I hope this book provided you with a starting place for answering your elder issues and concerns. Remember that nothing will replace consultation with a good elder law attorney who can address your specific situation and your specific concerns.

CHAPTER 19
MY ELDER JUST WENT TO THE NURSING HOME: WHAT SHOULD I DO NEXT?

PART OF OUR elder law practice involves helping people after a change of health, such as their parent or spouse having a medical downturn (stroke, fall, etc.) and going to the hospital. After a hospital stay, an elder is typically discharged to get rehabilitation in a skilled nursing facility. This is a very difficult and confusing time, which we call the "long-term care maze." Navigating this maze is difficult because:

- You have likely never done this before;
- You and your family may not be prepared (can you ever?);
- People (friends, family, neighbors) come at you with bad advice on things you should be doing;
- You are concerned about Medicare, Medicaid, powers of attorney and more; and
- You do not know what the next steps are.

So now that your loved one went to the hospital and is in the nursing home getting rehab, what questions should you be looking at?

- How long will they be there?
- What type of health insurance do they have?

- How expensive will rehab be?
- How are they responding to rehabilitation?
- Are the proper incapacity and estate planning documents in place?
- Should we apply for Medicaid?
- Will VA benefits help?
- What will happen next?

Let's discuss each of these questions in a little more detail:

HOW LONG WILL HE/SHE BE THERE?

Generally, the elder's ability to stay in rehabilitation is based upon their ability to get stronger and improve. The purpose of rehabilitation at this point is to get as strong as they can or to prevent further decline. At some point, whether through a decline in health, dementia or just general improvement, the elder's health insurance (i.e., Medicare or HMO) will stop paying for their stay in the rehabilitation facility.

WHAT TYPE OF HEALTH INSURANCE DO THEY HAVE?

This is very important as it may tell us how long the elder will be able to stay in rehab. The elder will likely either have Medicare with a supplement or a Medicare replacement policy (HMO or PPO). Medicare will pay up to 100 days of rehab with a co-pay of $167.50/day (2018) for days 21-100. The co-pays may be picked up by the Medicare supplemental policy depending on the Medigap plan; plans A and B do not cover the skilled nursing co-pay. An HMO or PPO will have a similar payment program based upon the individual policy. Generally, Medicare is more generous in allowing rehab days than HMOs. Regardless of health insurance, it is extremely rare that the elder will stay the full 100 days in rehab covered by their health insurance, which means now is the time to start planning on where they will go next. Learn more about Medicare and Long-Term Care here.

HOW IS THE ELDER RESPONDING TO REHABILITATION?

Health insurance only pays to get the patient stronger and will not pay if he or she is not willing to participate, is too sick, or cannot participate in rehab due to dementia. The family must work with the facility to make sure the elder is participating and getting stronger. If the elder cannot or will not participate in their therapy, for instance, the health insurance will stop covering the rehabilitation.

HOW MUCH WILL SKILLED NURSING COST?

The cost for skilled nursing will vary based upon the health insurance, but it can get very expensive if you are not working with the business office and social worker to keep track of how the elder is progressing, the type of health insurance, and other factors. When the health insurance (i.e., Medicare or the HMO) stops paying, the cost for long-term nursing care is between $250 to $300/day. When the health insurance stops paying for rehabilitation, this generally means that the elder is now in the skilled nursing facility for long-term care.

ARE THE PROPER INCAPACITY AND ESTATE PLANNING DOCUMENTS IN PLACE?

Now is definitely the time to make sure the elder has a last will and testament, durable power of attorney (done by an elder law attorney), designation of healthcare surrogate and living will. It may be time to update these documents if they are over 5 years old, or at least reviewed by an elder law attorney for accuracy, proper execution and relevance. Not all powers of attorney are created equal, for instance, and some do not allow the elder to protect their assets from the high cost of the nursing home.

WILL VA BENEFITS HELP?

A wartime veteran or his/her surviving spouse may be eligible for VA benefits when there are unreimbursed medical benefits. Please see our page on veteran's benefits and long-term care. At this point, it is likely that the VA will not help with nursing home/rehab costs, but it can never be too early to look for the veteran's military discharge paperwork, for instance. We can generally say that VA benefits will provide the most help when a veteran is trying to stay home or looking for help with the cost of an assisted living facility.

WHAT WILL HAPPEN NEXT?

When the rehabilitation portion ends, the elder has three choices:

1. Go home if they are well enough;
2. Go to an assisted living facility; or
3. Stay in the nursing home (very expensive!).

The ability to do any one of these may be very difficult. Will they be safe at home? Will Medicaid pay for home care? Will Veterans benefits help? What is the right facility? All of these questions, and more, are a part of the long-term care maze.

Importantly, our law firm is here to help you navigate the long-term care maze. With our health advocate on staff, we help make sure the elder is in the right place, getting the right care and then taking the next steps, through the maze, together.

SHOULD WE APPLY FOR MEDICAID?

This answer will depend on a number of factors such as where the elder goes next, their mental condition, their assets and their income. Now would be the time to meet with our law firm to make sure you are prepared to navigate the long-term care maze, protect assets, apply for benefits, and be prepared for will come next. Also, see the our list of Seven Lies Your Friends Tell You about Florida Medicaid.

WHAT ABOUT MOVING TO ASSISTED LIVING?

If the elder has been declining or may not be safe to go home, the family may want to take advantage of the elder's time in the nursing home and apply for Medicaid. Please read our report on obtaining Florida Medicaid for the assisted living facility. Veteran's benefits, such as "Aid and Attendance" may also be helpful in paying for your elder's assisted living facility as well.

When your elder has experienced a downturn in health, our law firm can help you answer all of these questions, and more, to make sure your elder gets the proper care, the assets are protected, and the family gets the help they need in making the right decisions.

WHERE CAN I GET GOOD HELP?

One of your first steps could be finding a good elder law attorney. One of the main points I make when helping families in difficult situations is that most people have never helped an elderly loved one. It is likely that a good elder law attorney can point you In the right direction for so many different things, and may provide a great deal of help before you realized you needed it.

GLOSSARY OF ELDER LAW TERMS

Accelerated Death Benefit

A life insurance policy feature that lets you use some of the policy's death benefit prior to death.

Activities of Daily Living (ADLs)

Basic actions that independently functioning individuals perform on a daily basis:

- Bathing
- Dressing
- Transferring(moving to and from a bed or a chair)
- Eating
- Caring for incontinence

Many public programs determine eligibility for services according to a person's need for help with ADLs. Many long-term care insurance policies use the inability to do a certain number of ADLs (such as 2 of 5) as criteria for paying benefits.

Acute Care

Recovery is the primary goal of acute care. Physician, nurse, or other skilled professional services are typically required and usually provided in a doctor's office or hospital. Acute care is usually short-term.

Adult Day Services

Services provided during the day at a community-based center. Programs address the individual needs of functionally or cognitively impaired adults. These structured, comprehensive programs provide social and support services in a protective setting during any part of a day, but not 24-hour care. Many adult day service programs include health-related services.

Adult Day Services

Services provided during the day at a community-based center. Programs address the individual needs of functionally or cognitively impaired adults. These structured, comprehensive programs provide social and support services in a protective setting during any part of a day, but not 24-hour care. Many adult day service programs include health-related services.

Advanced Directive

(also called Health Care Directive, Advanced Health Care Directive, Living Will, or Health Care Directive) Legal document that specifies whether you would like to be kept on artificial life support if you become permanently unconscious or are otherwise dying and unable to speak for yourself. It also specifies other aspects of health care you would like under those circumstances.

Alzheimer's Disease

Progressive, degenerative form of dementiathat causes severe intellectual deterioration. First symptoms are impaired memory, followed by impaired thought and speech, and finally complete helplessness.

Annuity

A contract in which an individual gives an insurance company money that is later distributed back to the person over time. Annuity contracts traditionally provide a guaranteed distribution of income over time, until the death of the person or persons named in the contract or until a final date, whichever comes first.

Assisted Living Facility

Residential living arrangement that provides individualized personal care, assistance with Activities of Daily Living, help with medications, and services such as laundry and housekeeping. Facilities may also provide health and medical care, but care is not as intensive as care offered at a nursing home. Types and sizes of facilities vary, ranging from small homes to large apartment-style complexes. Levels of care and services also vary. Assisted living facilities allow people to remain relatively independent.

Bathing

Washing oneself by sponge bath or in the bathtub or shower. One of the five Activities of Daily Living (ADLs)

Benefit Triggers (Triggers)

Insurance companies use benefit triggers as criteria to determine when you are eligible to receive benefits. The most common benefit triggers for long-term care insurance are:

1. Needing help with two or more Activities of Daily Living

2. Having a Cognitive Impairment such as Alzheimer's Disease

Caregiver

A caregiver is anyone who helps care for an elderly individual or person with a disability who lives at home. Caregivers usually provide assistance with activities of daily living and other essential activities like shopping, meal preparation, and housework.

Chronically Ill

Having a long-lasting or recurrent illness or condition that causes you to need help with Activities of Daily Living and often other health and support services. The condition is expected to last for at least 90 consecutive days. The term used in tax-qualified long-term care insurance policies to describe a person who needs long-term care because of an inability to do a certain number of Activities of Daily Living without help, or because of a severe cognitive impairment such as Alzheimer's Disease.

Cognitive Impairment

Deficiency in short or long-term memory, orientation to person, place and time, deductive or abstract reasoning, or judgment as it relates to safety awareness. Alzheimer's Disease is an example of acognitive impairment.

Community Spouse

Spouse of anursing home resident applying for or receiving Medicaid long-term care services.

Community-Based Services

Services and service settings in the community, such as adult day services, home delivered meals, or transportation services. Often referred to as home and community-based services, they are designed to help older people and people with disabilities stay in their homes as independently as possible.

Continence

Ability to maintain control of bowel and bladder functions, or when unable to maintain control of these functions, the ability to perform associated personal hygiene such as caring for a catheter or colostomy bag. This is one of the five Activities of Daily Living.

Continuing Care Retirement Communities (CCRC)

Retirement complex that offers a range of services and levels of care. Residents may move first into an independent living unit, a private apartment, or a house on the campus. The CCRC provides social and housing-related services and often also has an assisted living unit and an on-site or affiliated nursing home. If and when residents can no longer live independently in their apartment or home, they move into assisted living or the CCRC'snursing home.

Countable Assets

Assets whose value is counted in determining financial eligibility for Medicaid. They include:

- Vehicles other than the one used primarily for transportation
- Life insurance with a face value over $2,500
- Bank accounts and trusts
- Your home provided that your spouse or child does not live there and its equity value is greater than $572,000 (2018).

CPR (Cardiopulmonary Resuscitation)

Combination of rescue breathing (mouth-to-mouth resuscitation) and chest compressions used if someone isn't breathing or circulating blood adequately. CPR can restore circulation of oxygen-rich blood to the brain.

Custodial Care

Non-skilled service or care in the nursing home, such as help with bathing, dressing, eating, getting in and out of bed or chair, moving around, and using the bathroom. Also referred to as long-term care. Generally once Medicare/Rehabilitation ends.

Dementia

Deterioration of mental faculties due to a disorder of the brain.

Do Not Resuscitate Order (DNR)

Written order from a doctor that resuscitation should not be attempted if a person suffers cardiac or respiratory arrest. A DNR order may be instituted on the basis of an Advance Directive from a person, or from someone entitled to make decisions on the person's behalf, such as a health care proxy.

GLOSSARY OF ELDER LAW TERMS

In Florida this is printed only on yellow paper. Any person who does not wish to undergo lifesaving treatment in the event of cardiac or respiratory arrest can get a DNR order, although DNR orders are more common when a person with a fatal illness wishes to die without painful or invasive medical procedures.

Dressing

Putting on and taking off all items of clothing and any necessary braces, fasteners, or artificial limbs. This is one of the five Activities of Daily Living.

Durable Power of Attorney

Legal document that gives someone else the authority to act on your behalf on matters that you specify. The power can be specific to a certain task or broad to cover many financial duties. Your signature activates the documents; in Florida you cannot have the power of attorney activate on your unemployment. For the document to be valid, you must sign it before you become disabled.

Eating

Feeding oneself by getting food into the body from a receptacle or by a feeding tube or intravenously. It is one of the five Activities of Daily Living.

Elimination Period

(*also known as a Deductible Period or Benefit Waiting Period*) Specified amount of time at the beginning of a disability during which you receive covered services, but the policy does not paybenefits. A Service Day Deductible Period is satisfied by each day of the period on which you receive covered services. A Calendar Day or Disability Day Deductible Period doesn't require that you receive covered services during the entire deductible period, but only requires that you meet the policy's benefit triggers during that time period.

Equity Value

Fair market value of property minus any liabilities on the property such as mortgages or loans.

Estate Recovery

Process by which Medicaid recovers an amount of money from the estate of a person who received Medicaid. The amount Medicaid recovers cannot be greater than the amount it contributed to the person's medical care.

Exempt Assets

(also called Non-countable Assets) Assets whose value is not counted in determining financial eligibility for Medicaid. They include:

- Personal belongings
- One vehicle
- Life insurance with a face value under $2,500

Your home provided that its equity value is less than $572,000 (in Florida).

Federal Poverty Level

Income standard that the federal government issues annually that reflects increases in prices, measured by the Consumer Price Index.

Financial Eligibility

Assessment of a person's available income and assets to determine if he or she meets Medicaid eligibility requirements.

Functional Eligibility

Assessment of a person's care needs to determine if he or she meets Medicaid eligibility requirements for payment of long-term care services. The assessment may include a person's ability to perform Activities of Daily Living or the need forskilled care.

General Medicaid Eligibility Requirements

You must be:

- A resident of the state in which you are applying
- Either a United States citizen or a legally admitted alien
- Age 65 or over
- Or meet Medicaid's rules for disability, or blind
- Meeting certain asset and income guidelines

Health Care Surrogate

Legal document in which you name someone to make health care decisions for you if, for any reason and at any time.

Homemaker

Licensed Homemaker Services provides "hands-off" care such as helping with cooking and running errands. Often referred to as "Personal CareAssistants" or "Companions."

This is the rate charged by a non-Medicare certified, licensed agency.

Homemaker or Chore Services

Help with general household activities such as meal preparation, routine household care, and heavy household chores such as washing floors or windows or shoveling snow.

Hospice Care

Short-term, supportive care for individuals who are terminally ill (have a life expectancy of six months or less). Hospice carefocuses on pain management and emotional, physical, and spiritual support for the patient and family. It can be provided at home or in a hospital, nursing home, or hospice facility. Medicare typically pays for hospice care. Hospice care is not usually considered long-term care.

Incontinence

Inability to maintain control of bowel and bladder functions as well as the inability to perform associated personal hygiene such as caring for a catheter or colostomy bag. Continence is one of the six Activities of Daily Living.

Informal Caregiver

Any person who provides long-term care services without pay.

Instrumental Activities of Daily Living

Activities that are not necessary for basic functioning, but are necessary in order to live independently. These activities may include:

- Doing light housework
- Preparing and cleaning up after meals
- Taking medication
- Shopping for groceries or clothes
- Using the telephone
- Managing money
- Taking care of pets
- Using communication devices
- Getting around the community
- Responding to emergency alerts such as fire alarms

Living Will

(also called Advance Directive) Legal document that specifies whether you would not want to be kept on artificial life support if you become permanently unconscious or are otherwise dying and unable to speak for yourself. It also specifies other aspects of health care you would like under those circumstances and provides directions to your health care surrogate, family and medical personnel.

Long-Term Care

Services and supports necessary to meet health or personal careneeds over an extended period of time. Generally, the same thing as custodial care.

Long-Term Care Facility

(also called Long Nursing Home or Convalescent Care Facility) Licensed facility that provides general nursing care to those who arechronically illor unable to take care of daily living needs.

Long-Term Care Insurance

Insurance policy designed to offer financial support to pay for long-term care services.

Long-Term Care Services

Services that include medical and non-medical care for people with a chronic illness or disability. Long-term care helps meet health or personal needs. Most long-term care services assists people with Activities of Daily Living, such asdressing, bathing, and using the bathroom. Long-term carecan be provided at home, in the community, or in a facility. For purposes of Medicaid eligibility and payment, long-term care services are those provided to an individual who requires a level of care equivalent to that received in a nursing facility.

"Look Back" Period

Five-year period prior to a person's application for Medicaid payment of long-term care services. The Medicaid agency determines if any transfers of assets have taken place during that period that would disqualify the applicant from receiving Medicaid benefitsfor a period of time called the penalty period.

Medicaid

Joint federal and state public assistance program for financing health care for low-income people. It pays for health care services for those with low incomes or very high

GLOSSARY OF ELDER LAW TERMS

medical bills relative to income and assets. It is the largest public payer of long-term care services.

Medicare

Federal program that provides hospital and medical expense benefits for people over age 65, or those meeting specific disability standards. Benefits for nursing home and home health services are limited.

Medicare Supplement Insurance

(also called Medigap coverage) Private insurance policy that covers gaps in Medicare coverage.

Medigap Insurance

(also called Medicare Supplement Insurance) Private insurance policy that covers gaps in Medicare coverage.

Non-countable Assets

(also called exempt assets) Assets whose value is not counted in determining financial eligibility for Medicaid. They include:

- Personal belongings
- One vehicle
- Life insurance with a face value under $2,500
- Your home provided that your spouse or child lives there and its equity value is less than $572,000 (2018)

Nursing Home

(also called Skilled Nursing Facility, Rehabilitation or Long-Term Care Facility) Licensed facility that provides general nursing care to those who arechronically illor unable to take care of daily living needs. Generally reserved for the patients needing the most care.

Partnership Long-Term Care Insurance Policy

Private long-term care insurance policy that allows you to keep some or all of your assets if you apply for Medicaid after using up your policy's benefits. The Deficit Reduction Act of 2005 allows any state to establish a Partnership Program. Under a Partnership policy, the amount of Medicaid spend-down protection you receive is generally equal to the amount of benefits you received under your private Partnership policy. (State-specific program designs vary.)

Personal Care

(also called custodial care) Non-skilled service or care, such as help with bathing, dressing, eating, getting in and out of bed or chair, moving around, and using the bathroom.

Respite Care

Temporary care which is intended to provide time off for those who care for someone on a regular basis.Respite careis typically 14 to 21 days of care per year and can be provided in anursing home, adult day service center, or at home by a private party.

Reverse Mortgage

Type of loan based on home equity that enables older homeowners (age 62 or older) to convert part of their equity in their homes into tax-free income without having to sell the home, give up title, or take on a new monthly mortgage payment. Instead of making monthly payments to a lender, as you do with a regular mortgage, a lender makes payments to you. The loan, along with financing costs and interest on the loan, does not need to be repaid until the homeowner dies or no longer lives in the home.

Skilled Care

Nursing care such as help with medications and caring for wounds, and therapies such as occupational, speech, respiratory, and physical therapy. Skilled careusually requires the services of a licensed professional such as a nurse, doctor, or therapist.

Skilled Care Needs

Services requiring the supervision and care of a nurse or physician, such as assistance with oxygen, maintenance of a feeding tube, or frequent injections.

Spend Down

Requirement that an individual spend most of his or her income and assets to pay for care before he or she can satisfy Medicaid's financial eligibility criteria. As part of spend down, you can consult with an elder law attorney to help you protect assets.

Supplemental Security Income (SSI)

Program administered by the Social Security Administration that provides financial assistance to needy persons who are disabled or aged 65 or older. Many states provide Medicaid without further application to persons who are eligible for SSI.

Transfer of Assets

Giving away property for less than it is worth or for the sole purpose of becoming eligible for Medicaid. Transferring assets during the look back period results in disqualification for Medicaid payment of long-term care services for a penalty period.

Transferring

Moving into and out of a bed, chair, or wheelchair. Transferring is one of the five Activities of Daily Living.

ABOUT THE AUTHOR

D. "Rep" DeLoach III is a probate, estate planning and elder law attorney in Seminole, Florida. Rep DeLoach is Board Certified in Elder Law by the Florida Bar Association, a distinction earned by less than 1% of practicing attorneys. Rep is also VA Accredited. Practicing law since 1999, he is a popular speaker to both the public and to the legal community. A member of Wealth counsel and numerous estate planning and elder law organizations, Rep looks forward to helping you and your family plan your estate, protect your assets, and probate your loved one's estate, when necessary.

Please visit our website for more information and for a free copy of *The Top 20 Ways to Protect Your Florida Estate* and *The Florida Probate Process*, other books written by Rep DeLoach.

WA